Partnerships in Teacher Education

Schools and Colleges Working Together

Edited by
Thomas Warren
Beloit College

University Press of America
Association of Independent Liberal Arts Colleges for Teacher Education

Contents

iii

Foreword

Partnerships in Teacher Education, the final volume in AILACTE's four monograph series, provides excellent examples of the ways in which teacher education ultimately takes place within our public school partners.

I expect that this volume would have turned out quite differently had it been written just a few years ago. While AILACTE institutions have frequently been known for close alliances with those partners who help in the preparation of teachers, the mission, focus, and scope of those partnerships has undergone a remarkable transformation.

This shift has occurred in the midst of unparalleled conversation about the relationships between preservice teacher education, professional development of practicing teachers, and the achievement of children in the public schools. Goodlad (1990, 1994) presents evidence to suggest that we must consider the renewal of schools and teacher education simultaneously, looking to "centers of pedagogy" and "partner schools" as the structures and locations in which our work must occur. He suggests that only through new alliances among liberal arts faculty, teacher education faculty, and teachers in schools committed to renewal will we be able to refocus and renew our efforts to develop schooling that is responsive to its original purposes within our social and political democracy.

At the same time, the Holmes Group (1995) reported that "a good number of professors in schools of education must identify not only with their disciplines, but more actively with the public schools themselves. Research in the Education schools should be directed toward ground-breaking work on matters involving both the creation and the application of knowledge" (p. 17). Sykes (in press), suggests that the functions of this type of relationship are "pursuit of exemplary practice, facilitating changes in each partner institution, and creation of new capacity via learning." Howey (1995) contends that it will take the development of "persistent learning communities [as] . . . carefully planned arrangements [through which] certain key professional understandings and abilities can be acquired and refined."

So where does one turn for blueprints and frameworks for this kind of substantive change? What will be the assurances that this collaboration among partners will be substantive, creative, and purposeful? This book provides answers. The essays that follow are a rich and diverse collection that outline the nature of partnerships moving beyond the norm. The varied nature of the partnerships serves to confirm the notion that this is not a "one size fits all" endeavor. At the same time, the definition and development of such partnerships are within the reach of each of our institutions; and, as is often the case with AILACTE institutions, the stories contained herein are also stories of candor: efforts marked by successes and challenges.

Goodlad (1994, p. 166) reminds us that teaching is a fundamentally moral endeavor, with a clear need for each teacher to be a steward of the American schools. Stewardship of the school cannot happen without commitment on the part of all of those who train teachers to help new teachers understand how schools operate, why they are there to begin with, and how teachers continue to reflect upon and make decisions that are good for pupils and for the schools in which they work. This is a different lens through which beginners can view their own highly individual schooling experience. Partnerships like the ones described in this monograph should help each of us consider how teachers will be prepared for the future, particularly teachers of the growing number of children who do not currently view school as a meaningful part of their lives.

Greene (1995) believes that it will take imagination, in addition to careful thought and study, to see our way through the current problems facing American education. She says, "One of the reasons that I have come to concentrate on imagination as a means through which we can assemble a coherent world is that imagination is what, above all, makes empathy possible. It is what enables us to cross the empty spaces between ourselves and those we teachers have called 'other' over the years. ....That is because, of all our cognitive capacities, imagination is the one that permits us to give credence to alternative realities. It allows us to break with the taken for granted, to set aside familiar distinctions and definitions" (p.3.)

These essays will help readers see how imagination has already allowed AILACTE institutions to lead the way in forging new partnerships. Through their work, children from diverse backgrounds may also find a way to see rhyme, reason and imagination as important in their own lives.

References

Holmes Group (1995). *Tomorrow's schools of education.* The Holmes Group, Inc.

Howey, K. R. (1995, April). *The NBPTS core propositions: Implications for the laboratory and clinical preparation of preservice teachers.* Paper presented at the annual meeting of the American Educational Research Association. San Francisco.

Goodlad, J. I. (1994) *Educational renewal.* San Francisco: Jossey-Bass.

Goodlad, J.I., Soder, R., & Sirotnick, K.A. (Eds). (1990). *The moral dimensions of teaching. San Francisco: Jossey-Bass.*

Greene. M. (1995). *Releasing the imagination: Essays on education, the arts, and social change.* San Francisco: Jossey-Bass.

Sykes, G. (in press). Worthy of the name: Standards for the professional development school. In Levine, M. & Trachtman, R. (Eds.). *Building professional practice schools: Politics, practice, and policy.* New York: Teachers College Press.

Kathe Rasch, President
Association of Independent Liberal Arts Colleges for Teacher Education 1995-96.
Charlotte Mendoza, President
Association of Independent Liberal Arts Colleges for Teacher Education 1996-97.

Preface

Teachers can become isolated in their classrooms. It happens in primary grades, middle school, high school, and college. Isolation is not necessarily bad. Within the confines of private space, teachers can create and experiment free from the critical eyes of their peers. They can develop microcosms of outside worlds and strongly influence the rules within this tiny space. They can establish close relationships with their pupils. They can put a personal stamp on what happens as they teach and learn.

Similarly, institutions can become isolated in their buildings or on their campuses. It happens in elementary, middle, high schools, and beyond. Again, this is not necessarily negative. A dynamic, autonomous school can chart its own course. It can develop an ethos and tradition that makes it a singular force even though it may be officially linked to a district or system. A separate campus that is part of a far-flung university can develop uniqueness and personality that succeed where other campuses with similar resources fall short.

The opportunity to become autonomous is greater among independent liberal arts colleges than among governmentally supported counterparts. Independent liberal arts institutions should, can, and do go their own ways. Distinctiveness and individuality characterize their missions irrespective of the particular academic, religious, or ideological emphases that guide the curricula. Being able to operate individually as an institution can be a powerful advantage in times of reform or other rapid change.

However, the best offshoot of independence is not isolation. While teachers, schools, and colleges can benefit from their separateness, if they operate without a sensitive knowledge of what their kindred institutions are doing, they may not be able to be all that they can be. Knowing the agendas, activities, and aspirations of one's counterparts can only help in the relentless pursuit of excellence. If through knowing what others are doing, teachers expand their horizons and try something new, they will become more effective—capable of reaching and inspiring more students. If teachers, schools, or colleges find out from collaboration that they, themselves, are "the cutting edge" then they can rest peacefully . . . for a brief time until new challenges cry out for attention.

The point is this: Colleges have much to gain from collaboration.

The Association of Independent Liberal Arts Colleges for Teacher Education (AILACTE) was formed in 1980 to provide an effective network of communication, collaboration, and support among the independent liberal arts teacher preparation institutions across the United States. The Association has grown in number, influence, and complexity during the intervening years, and now has approximately two hundred fifty institutional members. Through annual meetings, periodic national forums, state affiliates, special interest groups, and publications, AILACTE helps to bring independent colleges and universities together for their mutual benefit and for the larger good of education.

AILACTE institutions must communicate with their fellow stake holders. The monograph series which concludes with this volume has sought to provide a vehicle for communication.

The first volume included sixteen original articles by presidents of liberal arts colleges. They articulated support for philosophies and programs that respond to the opportunities and challenges of teacher education. In that first preface I wrote "If teacher education in their midst is to succeed, [the presidents] must be supporters and constructive critics of it." Those sixteen presidents embodied these qualities. The first volume provided a rich collection of ideas "from the top." The various chapters have served as reference points for many AILACTE institutions. For example, Departments of Education have found support from their presidents via the words of other presidents. Presidents have learned from their counterparts.

The second monograph in the series acknowledged excellent teaching as a high priority within every AILACTE institution and taps into a priceless resource: The contribution of liberal arts and science professors from outside Departments of Education. These persons constitute a set of potential partners and partnerships. Whenever a faculty member of any department demonstrates effective teaching, it furthers the teacher education efforts of the institution, because students who are future teachers need to experience good teaching wherever it may be. Good teaching doesn't only take place in Departments of Education. By starting the monograph series with articles by presidents, AILACTE underlined the importance of and need for institutional support. Another kind of support is just as important if teacher education programs are to flourish: Namely, collegiality and mutual respect between educationists on the one hand and arts and science faculty on the other. The second book presented twenty original articles by liberal arts authors who were nominated to contribute because of their teaching excellence.

The third volume in the series included twenty-three articles by those persons who form the heart and soul of AILACTE: Faculty members in departments, colleges or schools of education. As the third volume's preface acknowledged, independent liberal arts colleges are not the only places in the United States where students can get excellent preparation for teaching, but the likelihood of success in these institutions is high, because their makeup and values so naturally support what teacher education needs. This conclusion is well-known and supported among the members of AILACTE, but it needs to be articulated in detail to wider audiences. Publicizing what we do was a major goal of the third volume which describes "promising practices": established programs and activities that help to make teacher education better on particular campuses.

The authors of each of the first three volumes stressed factors that define this uniquely American institution, the liberal arts college, and why it is best positioned to educate future teachers. This final monograph concentrates on why and how various constituents work together. The call for contributions gave the following instructions:

The fourth monograph to be published by AILACTE will feature partnerships between K-12 schools and our own AILACTE institutions. It follows the first in the series *A View from the Top: Liberal Arts Presidents on Teacher Education* ; the second, *A View from the Academy: Liberal Arts Professors on Excellent Teaching;* and the third, *Promising Practices: Teacher Education in Liberal Arts Colleges*. *Partnerships* is the concluding volume in this series.

Partnerships will feature efforts by AILACTE individuals, programs, departments, or institutions in cooperation with schools. The completed monograph will embody inclusiveness and variety rather than a narrow conception of partnerships. Consequently, it will consist of articles describing different types of relationships that are underway between individuals or groups in AILACTE institutions and colleagues in the schools. The emphasis is not on proposed efforts, but those that are already underway and succeeding. It will provide a sample of creative and effective cases of higher education working with the schools.

Here are some examples of types of partnerships that may be found in the monograph. Others are possible. A proposal should describe what happens in the partnership and why. A proposal will be expected to show why the particular partnership is creative, effective, and worthy of the national publicity and association with AILACTE that will come from its publication.

- An individual faculty member who works and contributes in both college and school settings.

- A college program that has had a significant influence on a school or district.

- A school program that has influenced the preparation of teachers.

- A team of faculty made up of members of both schools and higher education (teacher education and/or liberal arts faculty).

- A state or regional relationship with an AILACTE institution.

Many people contributed to the creation of this volume. The authors deserve the most credit. In seventeen of the twenty-one chapters, multiple writers collaborated. The membership and Executive Committee of AILACTE have been supportive from the start and deserve a special thank you. An editorial committee consisting of Deborah Norland of Luther College, Kathe Rasch[1] of Maryville University, and Julie Stoffels of Alverno College read every manuscript and worked with me to standardize and sharpen them as needed. At many campuses, articles and editorial comments were typed and corrected by secretaries and others who assisted in many ways. David Heesen, Head of the Beloit College Secretarial services, deserves a special mention for his many talents, attention to detail, and cheerful willingness to help throughout the publication of this series.

Thomas Warren
Beloit College
Publications Editor of AILACTE

---

1   Two of the three editorial committee members also co-authored articles. Their duties as members of the committee did not include making the acceptance decisions about their own work.

Introduction

Twenty-one stories about partnerships follow. They tell of efforts to reform, build bridges, enhance practice, and increase diversity. In every instance the number of *de facto* participating faculty members of a particular department or school increases because of the new relationships that are established. The number of available good ideas increases as well.

No author wants to return to what existed before the advent of the partnerships. "Once you collaborate, you never want to go back!" Such is the reaction of an elementary school teacher who is a partner of Kentucky Wesleyan College faculty members. Starting with a visit by the president of KWC to Cravens Elementary School several years ago as part of an effort to inject service leadership from the College into the community of Owensboro, this partnership has taught key lessons to its participants. Both the college and schools testify the benefits described in the article by Jo Tennison and Janice Hawes, .

A common question put forth by those college faculty who are not involved with partnerships asks, "How does a special relationship with schools get started?" Ralph W. Tyler, a 1922 graduate of Doane College would answer, "Ask the teachers what they want!" Picking up on this advice from an illustrious alum, the needs of P-12 educators have been the central focus of the partnership between Doane College and cooperating school personnel. Tyler's response to the question gives direction to help college teachers and students according to the article "Partnership for School Renewal: Site-Based Graduate Education Focusing on Individual School Needs" written by Kay Hegler and Richard Dudley of Doane.

Who are our partners? The short answer is no surprise to AILACTE member institutions: The partners are liberal arts and science faculty on our campuses and school teachers in the schools where we place our students. Educators will be able to explore the implications of such a question with elaboration and subtlety upon reading about a Missouri success story told by Kathe Rasch and Mary Ellen Finch of Maryville University.

The special role of arts and science faculty colleagues was featured in the second monograph in this series entitled *A View from the Academy: Liberal Arts Professors on Excellent Teaching*. While the present anthology concentrates on college and school relationships where the most active participants are teacher education faculty and school teachers, the role and presence of other professors also must be emphasized. Bringing school teachers into the faculty family as adjunct members formalizes relationships. The article entitled "Maryville College[1] and Secondary Educators: Linking Theory with Practice" by Marcia Keith & Terry Simpson describes a specific effort to bring new colleagues together to address common goals.

Many of the stories of partnerships began with a question embedded in some aspect of the reform movement. For example, how can the humanities maintain a strong presence in a state's educational priorities in the face of trends that run against humanities education? This was the challenge taken up by Madonna University through two projects supported by the National Endowment for the Humanities. The grants helped bring together liberal arts and education faculty within the university and link them to P-12 teachers in the nearby community. The chapter entitled "Only Connect! A Collaborative Project in the Humanities" by Marjorie Checkoway, Richard Sax, and Ernie Dolan tells how it was done.

A chapter by Alverno faculty members describes the case of a college's guiding principles and practice linking up with a school in search of self-renewal. A grant from the Joyce Foundation helped Alverno College and the Milwaukee Public Schools join forces to integrate performance-based authentic assessment into the teaching-learning process at middle and secondary schools. Julie Stoffels and Marguerite Sneed describe the results in their piece called "The Assessing Learning Project: Uniting Teacher Effectiveness and Student Learning."

Agents of change must themselves be open to new and surprising twists and turns, some of which may be initially troubling. In "Sowing Seeds of Transformation: Partnerships with a Purpose," Shannon Clarkson of Quinnipiac College distinguishes "transformation" from "reformation" where the former is a more graceful movement from the present to the future. For institutions without partnerships who want to develop them, the present often can be characterized by isolationism; the future, cooperation. More effective teacher education is a common goal of collaboration. Enriched schools and colleges emerge from the process.

---

1   Both Maryville COLLEGE (Tennessee) and Maryville UNIVERSITY (Missouri) provide chapters to this collection.

College/university partnerships are not only desirable, they are essential to teacher education according to Sharon Teets and Ronald Midkiff of Carson-Newman College. They wrote "Foxfire: Lighting the Way for Collaboration in Teacher Education." Formalized relationships, originally based on the individual involvement of higher education faculty in P-12 schools, are either strengthened or diminished by the manner in which the relationships develop. The chapter about Foxfire shows one fascinating process.

Too often teacher education that resides in colleges and universities separates higher education and P-12 efforts even though everyone acknowledges that both have key roles. Such a state of affairs has been a catalyst for the development of partnerships in general and this anthology in particular. A program at John Carroll University grew out of ongoing individuals' and organizations' relationships, and then engaged new participants in collaborative work and shared goals. "The Professional Education Model as a Catalyst for Reform and Renewal of a School-Based Program" is the title of the chapter by Kathleen Manning and Gerald Jorgenson of John Carroll.

Like that of many collaborative teacher education models, a goal of the partnership centered at Grinnell College is to learn from and build on the different perspectives of teacher education faculty and school teachers. Martha Voyles and her colleagues operated on the beginning assumption that open and thoughtful interaction should lead to mutual growth. Their chapter entitled "College-School Partnership to Improve Teacher Education" describes how the collaboration began and what has happened so far.

"Pre-Service Education in a Community of Practice" by Keith Campbell and Frederic Ross of Linfield College tells about a site-based secondary methods experience. The Linfield program provides a carefully thought out transition from the student's initial role in field experiences to a new professional position on the job as a student teacher. An emphasis is made to appreciate the especially significant learning that occurs as the student moves toward participation in professional practice. While cognitive factors, planning, and managerial skills of the student and cooperating teacher are important goals of a particular placement, the overall context of the placement also must be studied and nurtured.

Supervision of students in the field once was a major challenge to the faculty of Berry College in Georgia. Restructuring led to new relationships which empowered school and college teachers. This story is told via the chapter "Relationships as a Foundation: Emerging Field Experiences within Multiple College-School Partnerships" by Sam Hausfather, Mary Outlaw, and Elizabeth Strehle.

In "Race, Culture, and Power: A Collaborative Approach in Diversity Training and Educational Reform," Richard Biffle of Willamette University explores the interrelationship of culture and instructional practice. He asks a key question: "How can teachers help students understand and affirm their home and community cultures while also freeing them from the boundaries that these cultures may impose?"

The chapter by Charles Massey and Claity Price Massey entitled "Houghton College and the King Center School" describes the challenges confronting an isolated rural college with a homogeneous student population. The authors and others have developed a relationship with the King Center School in urban Buffalo, New York, which provides resources for both the college and the school. The use of computers and multi-media technology contribute significantly to the effort.

Partnerships in science and mathematics education is the topic of the chapter by Betty Tutt and Nancy Foley. They describe a project which grew out of Missouri's Outstanding Schools Act and an Eisenhower grant. The authors built a consortium which links a variety of partnerships within and between William Woods University and surrounding schools.

Girls and Women in Science is a time-tested partnership between Beloit College and cooperating schools. Supported by Eisenhower Mathematics and Science Education Program grants, the project brings together sixth grade girls and undergraduate women to promote investigative problem solving. Kathleen Greene tells about it in "The Beloit College Girls and Women in Science Project: Multiple Perspectives on Partnerships and Partnering."

"Running with the River: A Partnership Project Involving an Integrated Curriculum" describes communications and multi-media technologies as indispensable tools for facilitating interdisciplinary learning. This project grew out of a proposal to Ameritech from the teacher education faculty at the University of Findlay and colleagues in nearby schools. The focus is on a study of water, with the Blanchard River as a key resource. Natalie Abell, Melissa Cain, and Elizabeth Raker are the authors.

Emerging computer applications can be an entrée to new working relationships where the usual predictable knowledge base of students at a given age-level is turned on its head. Very young students can know so much about and do so much with electronic communications. College students (and faculty!) may not know or do much at all. In the chapter titled "Enhancing Teacher Education Through Collaboration: The Electronic Highway Connects College and Partner Schools," authors Mary Catherine Conroy, Lyle Jensen, Paula Bainbridge, and Rena Catron of

Baldwin-Wallace College show that a technological focus can benefit all participants through new emphases and expectations.

"Working Together Year-Round: A Teaching-Training Partnership" is written by Joseph Brown, Jimmie Russell, Judy Taylor, Michael Lackey, and Betty Chancellor of Oklahoma Baptist University. OBU and North Rock Creek Public Schools have joined into a collaboration which provides remedial and enrichment classes during the University's twice yearly intersessions. The intersession classes allow flexibility in teaching topics and working relationships between students and cooperating teachers.

A letter exchange between pre-service liberal arts teachers from Grand Canyon University and seventh grade pupils at an Arizona school formed the basis of a partnership in "authentic writing." The chapter "Pen Pals" by Joanna Jones and Kimberly Clem describes reactions from both age groups.

California suffers from a shortage of bilingual teachers. The College of Notre Dame has joined forces with a school district and local community to form a partnership that draws on the unique strengths of each partner. Diane Guay tells about it in her piece called "A Collaborative Program to Train and Certify Bilingual Teachers."

As you read these articles, communicate with the authors. Ask them what has happened lately. Give them your reactions to the chapters. Share your ideas which may help to make these excellent practices even better. Develop your ideas into an AILACTE Occasional Paper which will be distributed to all member institutions.

The Assessing Learning Project: Uniting Teacher Effectiveness and Student Learning

Julie Stoffels
Marguerite Sneed

Alverno College (Wisconsin)

Partnerships involving public school teachers and faculty from colleges of teacher education hold great promise for teaching and teacher education programs. The promise is greatest when the partners share a belief in the mutually-reinforcing nature of the work they do. Moreover, when the focus of the partnership is on ways in which the participants can work together to assure the success of all students, it can lead to what Goodlad (1994) calls educational renewal: "simultaneous renewal of schools and the education of educators" (p. 101).

There is increasing evidence in the field of education that the success of self-renewing schools is realized when the schools are "collaborative places where adults care about one another, share common goals and values, and have the skills and knowledge to plan together, solve problems together, and fight passionately but gracefully for ideas to improve instruction" (Garmston & Wellman, 1995, p.12). This approach to educational renewal requires movement away from highly-targeted innovations to systemic reform. Although school renewal necessitates recreating the organization from within, change occurs only when the institution supports continuous examination and improvement of the education process at every level. To achieve systemic reform at every level, then, those engaged in the process must acknowledge the need to involve higher education in the endeavor.

The purpose of this article is to describe a partnership between Alverno College and Milwaukee Public Schools (MPS), the Assessing

Learning Project, as a dynamic model of educational renewal. This project illustrates the positive change and renewal that can result when middle and high school teachers collaborate with college faculty to explore best practice and to discover the most effective ways to use that practice aimed at student success.

Introduction to the Assessing Learning Project

A promising aspect of school reform is the recognition that everyone engaged in teacher education must engage in a redesign process. At Alverno College, we view good teaching as building from a strong teacher preparation program, followed by a strengthening induction process, and continuing through ongoing staff development. Therefore, we have an interest in engaging in staff development processes of teachers beyond graduation to assist in this professionalizing process. Moreover, the education program at Alverno provides an added dimension to guiding the success of school reform through its focus on an assessment-as-learning process. Recognizing that learning goes beyond knowing to applying knowledge in meaningful contexts, Alverno faculty have designed a curriculum that resembles the focus of self-renewing schools on guiding students to meet broad-based standards of performance. Throughout their course work at Alverno, students practice applying their knowledge and abilities to meet the standards required of graduates. This assessment-as-learning process makes explicit what we want students to know and be able to do, gives them practice using the standards as a goal, and assesses their progress using multiple measures over time. For twenty years, Alverno has guided students in this process to successfully develop the skills, knowledge, and characteristics necessary for success.

To act on our desire to foster our involvement with public school reform, the Assessing Learning Project began in 1993 when Alverno College and Milwaukee Public Schools (MPS) joined forces under a grant from the Joyce Foundation. The project's objective is to support the large scale reform efforts of MPS through a focus on integrating performance-based authentic assessment into the teaching/learning process at the middle and secondary school levels. Two years earlier, an MPS curriculum initiative resulted in the development of ten K-12 Teaching/Learning Goals which guide the design of teaching/learning/assessment in the district. These broad-based Goals are at the heart of curriculum development in the district and guide the School Effectiveness Plans that principals have designed with teachers as a means of addressing the Teaching/Learning Goals.

2

This chapter details the evolution of the project, the changes and adaptations made along the way, and those characteristics which have emerged as supportive of systemic change. The project illustrates that those guiding the work of self-renewing schools are participating, not in just another fad that will go away, but in a fundamental shift in the way teachers teach and the way students learn.

The Evolution of the Assessing Learning Project

Initially the Assessing Learning Project provided a focus on developing and piloting writing portfolio assessment as a means to support Effectiveness Plans. During the 1991-92 school year, a comprehensive review of the district's city-wide assessments began in the areas of language arts and mathematics. In May 1992 the Milwaukee School Board mandated writing samples to replace multiple choice language tests in several grades. The Board also called for cross-curricular K-12 writing portfolios to be developed and piloted in 1992-93. Most Effectiveness Plans require a means of assessing student learning over time, a function that portfolios richly provide. The portfolios were to be used to describe children's K-8 performance and would become part of the graduation standards in high school. Performance and portfolio assessments were also piloted in mathematics. Having pioneered performance-based assessment among its own students, Alverno College is viewed as a national leader in discussions of assessment reform. Since faculty from the college had worked closely with MPS in its K-12 teaching/learning reform, the School Board's mandate triggered a more formal initiative to create a partnership in order to advance educational renewal.

To fund the project, Alverno and MPS submitted a proposal to the Joyce Foundation for a two-year grant. The grant was awarded and the project began in June 1993. (Subsequently Joyce renewed the grant for a second two years.) There were three primary goals in effect:

- To provide the MPS district with a more rigorous and appropriate measure of student success in writing by involving middle and high school teachers in developing and piloting a writing portfolio assessment;

- To develop a team of teachers at each middle and high school knowledgeable about performance-based assessment and capable of working with students and other members of the staff; and

- To strengthen the district's emphasis on the development of strong communication skills in young people.

During the first year, context was set for the project through an inservice session for principals on instructional/assessment alignment. In MPS, principals are held accountable for the achievement of students at their schools, so the involvement of principals in this project is viewed as crucial to the goals of the project. This inservice session, led by Alverno faculty, detailed local, state, and national directions in assessment and introduced performance-based authentic assessment. Some principals planned and initiated involvement in the project as a result of this initial input session. Other principals chose to wait to involve their teachers at another point in time judged by them to be more opportune to the reform work in that individual school.

Significant adaptations have been made during the course of the first three years of the Assessing Learning Project. These adaptations have emerged from ongoing evaluation of the impact of the project on individual schools, on teams in those schools, and on teachers in the teams. They have also resulted from the evaluation by facilitators and coordinators of the summer institutes.

Primary Stages in the Assessing Learning Project

The four primary stages guiding the work of the Alverno faculty and MPS staff to meet partnership's goals are:

- Making an Initial School Contact;

- Planning for the Summer Institute;

- Facilitating and Participating in the Summer Institute Session; and

- Following Up With Summer Institute Participants.

These stages emerged gradually over the first year and stimulated a process within the project that has evolved over the course of the partnership. The stages themselves provide a map to guide the work of the project and serve as points of comparison for subsequent planning from year to year. They also represent a process which supports the simultaneous renewal of teachers, teacher educators, and teacher initiates.

Making an Initial School Contact

The first stage of the process is to make contact with schools that have not yet taken advantage of the opportunity to become involved in the Assessing Learning Project. With the assistance of the facilitators and MPS staff, the Alverno faculty who follow up with participant teams during the academic year also plan a contact strategy for involving new

4

teams for the upcoming summer institute. Principals who express an interest in having their school be involved in the project request that presentations be given during the spring by a team of Alverno faculty working with MPS facilitators and participants from the previous summer institute. The MPS facilitators/participants provide an important dimension of credibility to the presentation for the audience of classroom teachers. The purpose of the presentation is to show the project's connections to initiatives already being undertaken at the school and to the MPS Teaching/Learning Goals. Since the goal of the project is eventually to involve every middle and high school in a summer institute session, Alverno faculty and MPS teachers and principals keep that eventuality in mind as they work together on other initiatives in the district such as School to Work and Equity 2000, federal programs to support reform. An incentive for participants is that they can earn two graduate credits for the summer institute course and an additional credit for continuing to be involved in the follow-up process.

Planning for the Summer Institute

The second stage of the process is planning for a summer institute. The planning team consists of Alverno faculty and staff members from MPS. A consensus model is employed to guide the planning process. Coordinators, from Alverno and from MPS, lead the team planning of the summer institute based on four goals of the project. The focus of each day's work in the institute thus becomes centered upon these goals, which are to guide participants to:

- Develop understandings of strategies for performance assessment based on the relationships among teaching, learning, and assessment;

- Integrate teaching/learning goals that serve as standards by which teachers both create instruction and assess student learning;

- Develop confidence, through integrating teaching/learning goals in the design of the assessment process, to assist students in becoming more self-directed and responsible for their own learning;

- Participate in building a learning community of teachers knowledgeable about performance assessment and capable of working with colleagues in their schools to implement an organizational plan to sustain improved teaching and learning.

The summer institute agenda is constructed to provide a balance between input on the assessment process from the institute facilitators and time for teams to meet together separately to work toward meeting the institute goals. In addition to the broad goals indicated above, teams are asked to identify more explicit goals for their work together.

The role of the institute planners begins early in the fall following the August summer institute. At that time, the facilitators of the previous summer institute meet to evaluate the session, deciding what worked well and why, what needed changing, and what should be added to the next summer's session. Recommendations are elicited from facilitators for names of teacher participants who would be good facilitator candidates for the following summer. By February, a new team of facilitators for the upcoming institute is chosen and invited to help plan the sessions for August.

Facilitating and Participating in the Summer Institute

The two-week summer institute comprises the third stage of the process. Its main features are the content focus, the use of facilitators, reflective journals, and a model classroom. The content focus varies according to the needs of the participants. In the first year of the project, the focus was on communication, particularly in the area of writing across the curriculum. As teachers' needs and district requirements changed and evolved, the summer institute participants responded. For example, in the second summer, participants requested explicit exposure to and practice with portfolios and other assessment tools. By the third year, participants requested more information on how to articulate expectations of performance to students and how to evaluate those performances with an emphasis on helping students to continue to develop ways to assess their own performances.

Each team (nine the first year, eight the second, and nine the third) works directly with a facilitator from the institute planning team. The facilitator—an Alverno faculty member or an MPS teacher or staff member—sees her/his role as both supporting and initiating progress toward the goals the team has identified. Facilitators are trained to focus on helping the team to problem solve important issues, to discover resources helpful to their work together, and to gain confidence in their ability to accomplish their goals as a team when they return to their school at the start of the school year.

Reflective journals are directive in nature, asking participants to reflect on the focus of the day and to relate it to her/his own experience and understanding. They become a rich resource for the facilitator who gives daily feedback on the entries themselves and detailed summary feedback to each participant at the conclusion of the two-week institute. Journals are equally as important for the participant, who can return

6

to her/his thoughts both during the summer institute and when the new academic year gets under way and feel renewed by being reminded of the change focus they agreed to keep with their team.

A model classroom of 20 to 25 middle-school age students is team taught by two MPS teachers using an interdisciplinary focus that employs the same assessing learning techniques being presented in the institute. Observation time is built into the schedule of the teams/participants so that they can observe what teaching and assessing look like in a classroom that integrates the MPS Teaching/Learning Goals as standards by which the teachers assess student learning.

Following Up With Summer Institute Participants

The final stage of the process is a year-long follow-up with participants which begins with facilitator feedback. Following the Assessing Learning Project summer institute, each facilitator of the individual teams sends written feedback (1) to the team as a whole regarding their social interaction as a group, and (2) to each individual on the team. This feedback provides another model of assessment that participants can duplicate in their classrooms. An example of feedback given to a team illustrates the typical nature of its detail:

> It was heartening to see the evolution of your group over the two weeks of the institute. While some of you expected a different type of learning process than the one we guided you through, you were able to grow in your understanding not only of performance assessment, but also of non-linear, constructivist approaches to learning. We believe, with developmental psychologists like Gardner, that the effort it took to construct new meanings will help you to make the experience of the summer institute a powerful influence on your practice.
>
> You have made some solid plans to build on the experience of the summer institute. As you probably understood from my comments during the institute, I'd encourage you not to be too wary in inviting others to explore the principles of assessment and the process of thinking anew about teaching and learning. Your awareness of the link between meaningful instruction and meaningful assessment is strong—share it! Your own experience of needing to make your understandings concrete can also guide you in your relationships with the faculty. When you have examples of assessment as learning in your own classrooms, find ways to share them. Let us know how we can assist you with that.

7

As illustrated in the team feedback above, the feedback to individuals also provides a balance of support for change and suggestions for continued challenge. For example:

> Throughout your reflective journal it is clear that, as a teacher, you feel responsible for continuing to develop your abilities and to find ways to assist students to grow. I especially liked your question, "How do I get off to a 'bang-up' start?" You entered into the work of your team with enthusiasm and participated actively.

> I have a sense from your journal that you have a gift for creating effective assignments/assessments. The description of writing to show learning (The Smell of Fruit) is one example. Let me encourage you to keep an ongoing collection of samples that you can share with other teachers (and with fieldwork students and student teachers from Alverno, too!).

The most sustaining aspect of the follow-up process in the Assessing Learning Project is the school visits that Alverno faculty make regularly following a team's participation in the summer institute. The nature of these visits varies from school to school and is based on individual needs of former participants. The team meets with Alverno representatives to share the work they have done since returning to school and to project ways that Alverno coordinators might help to sustain the changes that individuals have begun. The coordinators also encourage teams to present their work at teachers' meetings and to involve other colleagues in the team's focus. This staff-development focus provides an ongoing emphasis on developing teacher-initiated goals and activities that result in sustainable teacher change.

What the Assessing Learning Project Has Taught Us

Michael Fullan (1990) has taught educators/reformers to understand that we need both reason and opportunity to change. By joining forces through the Assessing Learning Project, MPS and Alverno provide teachers and administrators with support for systemic change. Several key aspects of our collaboration have energized the process. Alverno had the initial invitation from the district to join them in the reform efforts they had begun through devising Teaching/Learning Goals, and both partners had an expectation for the Goals to be implemented. The district provided the authority to guide teachers to think about teaching/learning in new and creative ways; and flexibility to implement change was built in at the building level by involving the principal, or administrative representative, in the process. The experience of Alverno faculty provided access to knowledge. The summer institute provided the forum for dialogue. It also provided a framework for teachers to think differently about how they teach and how students learn and to translate their new-found understanding into designing their teaching differently. Then, MPS district leadership encouraged building principals to provide time during the school year for ongoing staff development around issues of teaching/learning/assessing and for continuous interaction among colleagues that was modeled in the summer institute.

Throughout the three years of the Assessing Learning Project, we have evaluated, redesigned, and adapted its components in an ongoing and collaborative way. As a result, we have developed an appreciation for, and a degree of expertise in, ways to create a successful partnership for change. There are three elements in particular that have been most instructive to us in the success of the Assessing Learning Project: facilitating change, connecting classroom practice with teacher education, and sustaining innovation.

Facilitating Change

Initially, Alverno faculty were the core leaders in the project. They guided the work of the first summer institute, designing its focus and training MPS personnel to take on some of the leadership tasks. It became apparent during the first year of follow-up, however, that many of the teachers who were participants that first summer were themselves valuable resources for encouraging teachers attending subsequent institutes. They had insights, experience, enthusiasm, and the ability to communicate effectively about the new approaches to teaching and learning they had developed and implemented in their classrooms through the two-week institute. Therefore, we asked these teachers to accompany us when we gave invited presentations to potential project participants. Alverno faculty gave an overview of the project and the teachers provided support for its success through their sharing of the strategies/materials they created and classroom examples of their students' work. Audience response and interaction with the participant teachers at these meetings were very positive.

Because of their motivating influence and developing expertise in changing their teaching in the classroom, we further invited the former participant teachers to serve as facilitators for the next summer institute. Alverno faculty, MPS central office personnel, and the participant facilitators now work together to plan the next summer institute. We assign facilitators to participating teams according to a mutual assessment of the strengths of the facilitator and the strengths and needs of the team. To refine and enhance the success of grass-roots facilitating of the process, we have also instituted a formal facilitator training component, which provides practice for the facilitators to gain confidence in their ability to guide change. The lesson learned is that bottom-up or grass roots facilitating is often more successful than top-down delivery.

To further reinforce the training of facilitators, MPS teacher participants in the project have accompanied Alverno faculty to national conferences—the American Association of Higher Education (AAHE), the American Association for Colleges of Teacher Education (AACTE), and the Association of Independent Liberal Arts Colleges for Teacher Education (AILACTE)—to co-present the work of the Assessing Learning Project. In addition to enhancing facilitation/presentation skills, their involvement has served both to cement their own focus on change in their classrooms (an input) and to provide real impetus to conference audiences for pursuing school/college partnerships (an added outcome).

Connecting Classroom Practice and Teacher Education

Alverno faculty—as a result of their intense involvement in helping public school teachers to engage in change and to focus on assessing as learning—have adapted their own teaching and classroom practice. We have learned to assist teacher initiates to understand characteristics of school/college partnerships and how to foster such collaboration in the schools in which they practice. Within courses, Alverno faculty promote interdisciplinary teaching/learning. Students are given information on the MPS Teaching/Learning Goals and on the many reform initiatives in MPS. Their field work experiences provide opportunities to experience the components of those initiatives and their relationships to supporting the goals. Students are also given opportunities to experience components of the change process and to interact with Assessing Learning Project teacher participants as guest panelists in Alverno classrooms.

Within the education program at the college, experience with the project has led us to restructure secondary education methods courses to include an interdisciplinary component. We have also begun the design of a separate program focused on middle school teaching.

Assessing Learning Project teacher participants have become cooperating teachers for Alverno field students and student teachers. Together the students and cooperating teachers are discovering workable ways to infuse performance assessment into the classroom and to facilitate the learning of all students through focusing that assessment on the Teaching/Learning Goals. In addition, summer institute participants are encouraged to become trained external assessors of our students at Alverno. For example, they are invited to learn to judge student performance in social interaction, a process that is an integral component of the summer institute experience. In this way, the partnership, a single connection for school reform, has led to many interconnection opportunities that serve to sustain the innovation in both institutions.

Sustaining Innovation

During the past three years, participants in the Assessing Learning Project have developed a set of critical success factors for creating and maintaining successful school/college partnerships.

- Collaboration among all levels of leadership and power in the endeavor: Unless all constituents view one another as colleagues with a common desire to help all students become successful learners, the risk-taking necessary to change the way we view teaching and learning cannot occur.

- Negotiation of time and resources: These are necessary to meet the changing needs both of teachers who participate in the project and of those who become influenced by them to seek new opportunities for supporting greater student success.

- Tolerance for ambiguity among all constituents: This recognizes that elements of successful change are non-linear and unpredictable.

- Investment in the belief that all students can learn, an investment that is both individual and group-based: Teachers and administrators must work together to help students see that they learn best when they are expected to take responsibility for their learning.

- Development to high standards of accomplishment: School personnel must also be devoted to accomplishing high levels of success through giving students explicit expectations for learning, access to knowledge and performance that illustrates both acquisition and application of that knowledge, feedback on student success in meeting those expectations, and ongoing support and guidance in the process.

By embracing these critical success factors, participants in the project acquire a sense of moral purpose and a renewed and refined commitment to guiding student learning. The result is that the locus of leadership shifts to the classroom teacher as the primary influence on the success of students. It is this classroom-based leadership, not mandates from above, that provides the basis for successful and ongoing change.

A continuing emphasis on the nature of change itself can be helpful in the college's support of systemic reform. Such an emphasis helps all participants in the reform efforts to come to believe that positive change can take place and that change is a good thing. Participants learn not to undertake change for the sake of change alone, but because the project has provided ample evidence that students do in fact take on responsibility for their own learning when teachers set high standards and guide students to meet them. Consequently, teachers develop a confidence that their newly-found skills and abilities around the assessing-as-learning focus actually are helping them to meet the diverse needs of their students.

The Assessing Learning Project has become structured to recognize that individuals and systems must come together to structure reform. Furthermore, everyone involved in the endeavor must together adopt a set of common goals toward which they are striving and on which they can judge their progress. Such collaboration requires that teachers and administrators work as trustworthy colleagues. As a result, and to sustain change in a positive way, administrators have moved away from judging teachers in traditional ways as they struggle with change, instead focusing on the positive processes and outcomes toward changes they are attempting to achieve. Moreover, all administrators in a successful participating school support change and believe that their teachers are the best ones to achieve it.

Above all, the partnership must maintain frequent and open communication both during the summer institute and throughout the school year. Support for change comes not only in the classroom but also in the hallways where students, teachers, and administrators interact and through school policies that determine consequences for student behavior, both social and antisocial. Support must also come through college programs preparing teachers to teach in that atmosphere.

Conclusion

The project is a success in that it endures as an active partnership between college and schools and enjoys enthusiastic support from both communities. The project has succeeded because it expresses both the ambition and determination to create and nurture the passion to achieve educational renewal through the professional development of teachers. It is a success because teachers and college faculty work together on matters of common concern, acknowledging the primacy of classroom teachers in the teaching/learning process, and the dependence upon them as necessary change agents. Ultimately, the success of the project will be measured by the degree to which the partnership achieves its overarching goal: that students develop and express the understanding and abilities they need in order to respond to and shape the world in which they live.

Notes

1. In performance-based authentic assessment, a student demonstrates specific behaviors and abilities in a situation much like that encountered in real life. For example, if an education student is being assessed on her ability to clearly and accurately present a new curriculum idea to the school board, she is asked to give a speech for that purpose to a real or imagined audience composed of school board members.

References

Fullan, M. (1990). Staff development, innovation, and institutional development. In B. Joyce (Ed.), *Changing school culture through staff development* (pp. 3-25). Alexandria, VA: Association for Supervision and Curriculum Development.

Garmston, R. & Wellman, B. (1995). Adaptive schools in a quantum universe. *Educational Leadership 52* (7), 6-12.

Goodlad, J. (1994). *Educational renewal: Better teachers, better schools.* San Francisco: Jossey-Bass Publishers.

Enhancing Teacher Education Through Collaboration: The Electronic Highway Connects College And Partner Schools

Mary Catherine Conroy, Lyle C. Jensen
Paula Bainbridge, Rena Catron

Baldwin-Wallace College (Ohio)

Designing an effective school-college partnership is contingent upon professors reaching out to establish a dialogue with school administrators and teachers. This willingness to involve teachers and administrators in the preparation of future teachers recognizes the credibility, the expertise, and the experience that practitioners contribute to this important work. Traditionally the talents and expertise of this vital group of professionals have gone unrecognized. These voices must be heard by college professors if the teacher education curriculum is to prepare future teachers for the realities of today's classroom.

Planning initiated by two college professors with principals from local schools has given instructional technology a new perspective in teacher education at Baldwin-Wallace College in Berea, Ohio. The need to collaborate with teachers and administrators in the field was first seen individually by the college professors. The initiative was driven by the professors' experience as practitioners in educational leadership partnerships programs which predisposed them to reach out to schools and break with the traditional view held by college professors who isolate themselves from the realities classroom teachers face throughout the United States. This action resulted in a joint decision to design a strategy which would identify school administrators willing to develop

14

a collaborative partnership that would be mutually beneficial for pre-service teachers, classroom teachers, and their students.

Based on the Baldwin-Wallace College professors' work with the greater community, two school principals were identified and agreed to take a risk and join them in planning a college-school initiative which enhanced teacher education while meeting their needs. The design promoted genuine collaboration and provided an opportunity where shared visions translated into effective and significant programs. The success of this highly interactive process has been based upon mutual professional commitment, trust, perseverance, effective communication, and the willingness to change.

As a result of this dialogue that involved many meetings at the local schools and college, the Baldwin-Wallace College - Berea City Schools Partnership was initiated. It was agreed that a technological focus would benefit all partnership participants: the college student, the classroom teacher, the college professor, school administrator, and especially the student within the elementary classroom.

The importance of computer technology in the learning environment and how the role of the teacher changes is best described by Peter Drucker:

> There are more hours of pedagogy in one thirty-second commercial than most teachers can pack into a month of teaching. The subject matter of the TV commercial is quite secondary; what matters is the skill, professionalism, and persuasive power of the presentation. Children, therefore, come to school today with expectations that are bound to be disappointed and frustrated. They expect a level of teaching competence that goes beyond what most teachers can possibly muster. Schools will increasingly be forced to use computers, television, films, videotapes, and audio tapes. The teacher increasingly will become a supervisor and a mentor—much, perhaps, the way he functioned in a medieval university some hundreds of years ago. The teacher's job will be to help, to lead, to set examples, to encourage; it may not primarily be to convey the subject matter itself. (Drucker, The New Realities, 249).

Today the computer is used by many teachers as one tool that helps them to create classrooms that encourage active learning, cooperative learning, and enables teachers to individualize lessons.

The partnership design took into consideration specific needs of both the school district and the college. The Berea City Schools were undergoing rapid change and reform that included introduction of technology into the classrooms. Each elementary school in the system opened the 1994-95 school year with a new library/media center and Macintosh computer lab and accompanying software. The two schools involved in the partnership with Baldwin-Wallace College, Parknoll Elementary and Riveredge Elementary, had additional technological needs. Parknoll was interested in using its new computer lab to enhance the curriculum of children in kindergarten through grade five. The IBM Writing to Read Lab was an integral part of the primary language instruction program. Both labs presented a situation where the school had available technology but needed assistance with the planning and supervision which would be necessary for the successful integration of the new technology into the daily curriculum. Riveredge Elementary opened the 1994-95 school year with forty Macintosh computers in four labs throughout the building which were networked using the Jostens curriculum software. This along with twenty existing computers in the school as well as a primary Writing to Read Lab presented a number of challenges to the staff that included: how to integrate the technology into the daily curriculum and instruction, and also how to identify resources in the community to assist and support technology integration.

The Division of Education faculty at Baldwin-Wallace College recognized the need for students to have a knowledge of computer technology and required them to take an Educational Technology and Computer Literacy course as part of their preservice education curriculum. The Division of Education also acquired a state-of-the-art Power Macintosh/CD Rom computer lab in 1994 with direct access to the internet and laser disk technology which moved the course beyond the Apple II stage. This technological update led to the need to reexamine the course design. Initially the technology course did not involve a field experience component; however, the partnership initiative created an on-site field experience opportunity. The redesign required considerable planning since numerous details, such as schedules and transportation, had to be taken into account at both the college and school site. As a component of the redesign, the college professors in collaboration with the teachers planned an evaluation of the students' field experience.

This collaborative planning resulted in a course which included not only classes in the college computer lab, but six site visits working directly with the teacher using computer technology in the classroom. This was followed by the student writing two reflective papers evaluating the interaction that took place within the technology-rich classroom which involved the student applying theory to their classroom observations. Students also developed a technology portfolio comprised of lesson plans, utilized software applications and the Internet, and prepared a demonstrated classroom lesson integrating computer technology as a teaching/learning tool. The course also involved student discussion sessions focusing on their analysis of children's behavior while using technology and the interaction between the classroom teacher and the child.

The reflective papers written by the college students indicated successful transfer of theory to practice. As one insightful student commented:

> . . . as a student I have used computers primarily as a word processor for writing papers. Now that I am aspiring to become a teacher I am looking for more ways to use computers in class. To me the most significant part of this project was speaking to the teacher who is already familiar with computers in this setting. I now feel sure they are a very necessary part of the curriculum because the computer is a tool. The computer also enables the teacher to access, analyze, and manage information that enhances learning.

Another student, after reading one of her required readings, *The Children's Machine* by Seymour Papert, agreed that as the world races down the "information super highway it is important our children not travel in the slow lane." The challenge for preservice teachers is to become more aware of the ever-changing technology that is available to classroom teachers.

Another outcome of the field experience was advice received by one student from the partner teacher regarding interviewing for a teaching position. She suggested questions a teacher candidate should ask, such as: "How computer-advanced is your school system? How are you implementing computer technology in the classroom? What are your plans for teacher-training and staff development regarding computer use in the classroom?"

As a result of the technology partnership program, teachers and administrators were able to use the college students' talents and provide a more individualized learning environment for their students in a computer-assisted instruction environment. The teachers also could plan on this assistance throughout the school year. Previously teachers and principals could not do long-term planning that involved college students because during some academic quarters they would have students, while during other quarters they would not. Schools had never been consulted concerning when they could best use college students. Field experience schedules were typically made for the convenience of the college rather than for the needs of the school.

The willingness of the two college professors to visit the schools, meet with the staff, and discuss curriculum design opened communication and provided a vehicle to continue the conversation of collaboration for the purpose of future initiatives. This paradigm shift from isolation to

17

collaboration in the way professors, teachers, and principals communicate and interact is necessary if higher education is to be responsive in
effectively preparing future teachers for the technology enhanced curriculum.

The technology partnership program also enabled other initiatives
to unfold. For example, students in the Educational Technology Course
participated in an electronic mail (E-mail) project with a local high
school. The project was initiated by inviting an English teacher and
two of his students to the college class to explain how the project would
work. The tenth graders had the opportunity to speak to college students and discuss a research project they were working on as well as
explore the new Baldwin-Wallace College computer lab. Then preservice students reviewed research outlines for tenth graders via E-mail.

After working out the details of getting a college E-mail account for
the high school students and their teacher, the project was launched.
Preservice teachers were to act as friendly critics to the high school
sophomores who were involved in writing activities: research, use of
quotations, making comparisons, analyzing, and evaluating. The
Baldwin-Wallace students had to make sure outlines created by their
high school partners had meaning, authority, voice, development, design
and clarity. Once the high school students completed their outline they
sent it to the preservice teachers via E-mail. After reviewing the
outlines the preservice teachers E-mailed their responses back to the
high school. The experience of using E-mail was best summarized by
one preservice student:

> I think that using E-mail in the curriculum is a good way to
> encourage students to gain information from other schools. I
> liked having college students interact with younger students,
> especially using E-mail. The use of electronic mail is a tool
> that teachers can use to connect their students to a city or even
> another country.

Through the technology partnership program, college professors
invited teachers to the campus to address topics, including: inclusion,
teaming, proficiency testing, management styles, and parent-teacher
communication. In turn, the college faculty were invited to participate
in school staff development programs related to current issues and
trends.

Several conclusions can be drawn from the successful college-school
technology site collaboration. All constituents need to be directly involved in the decision-making throughout the process and that, in
addition to time, requires flexibility, and frequent meetings to plan.
Professors need to be willing to go to the school site and talk with

administrators and teachers rather than requiring that everything take place on the college campus. This type of partnership leads to a new level of interaction between college professors and classroom teachers. Everyone benefits.

This partnership that began at the personal level between the college professors and principals and teachers has worked its way through the hierarchial structure of both organizations. Enthusiasm has been generated that now involves the president of the college and the superintendent of schools in planning further partnership initiatives. The initiatives include the decision for the college and school district to share financial resources, to install an fiber-optic network to connect schools in northeastern Ohio, as well as to adjust personnel policies that include the sharing of a staff person to direct an enrichment center within a partner school.

This computer technology partnership venture provides a unique model of what can happen when two professors and two school principals challenge the traditional hierarchical view of how schools and colleges view one another. All too often higher education is viewed as the top of a pyramid that is supported by a structure made up of the primary, elementary, middle, and secondary schools.

Preparing future teachers for the challenging classrooms that exist nationally takes the involvement of all members of the education community.

Viable college-school partnerships need to be planned, organized, and continually assessed as they take form. It is critical that such collaborative efforts be given adequate time to grow, evolve, and become established. If mandated programmatic components or rigid expectations are prematurely imposed upon beginning initiatives, the partnership may be doomed.

Partnership relationships require an investment of planning time and concentrated effort if they are to evolve into responsive and successful programs. The challenge to teacher education faculty as they prepare future teachers for classrooms equipped with computer technology was described by Vartan Gregorian, President of Brown University:

> The relevant organizational structures must change to adopt the new technology and until that happens the real technology revolution in higher education will not have occurred. This was the case of the printing press, the Industrial Revolution, the automobile, air travel, and radio and television. The new technology per se is not a revolution—the revolution is how we organize, structure and empower our lives (HIERA, 1992).

The willingness to break with current teacher education practices and the commitment of two neighboring educational institutions has created a climate of collaboration in Berea, Ohio. Baldwin-Wallace College and the Berea City Schools have shared not only the electronic highway, but they have shared a vision and a commitment to make a difference in the preparation of teachers and in the lives of their students.

References

Drucker, Peter (1992). *The new realities: In government and politics, in economics and business, and in society and world view.* New York: Harper & Row.

Fisher, Charles, Wilmore, Faye, and Howell, Robert (Winter 1993-94). Classroom technology and the new pedagogy. *Journal of Research on Computing in Education.* 26 (2), 220-236.

Laszlo, A. and Castro, K. (1995). Technology and values: Interactive learning environments for future generations. *Educational Technology.* 35 (2) 7-12.

Marcinkiewicz, Henryk (1994). Computers and teachers: Factors influencing computer use in the classroom. *Computing and Teacher Education.* 26 (2), 220-236.

Papert, Seymour (1993), *The children's machine: Rethinking schools in the age of the computer.* New York: Basic Books.

Schrum, Lynne (1994). First steps into the information age: Technology infusion in a teacher education program. *Journal of Computing and Teacher Education.* 10 (4), 12-14.

Vartan, Gregorian, Taylor, Merrily, & Hawkins, Brian L. (1992). What presidents need to know about the integration of information technology on campus. In *Higher Education Information Resource Alliance: Executive Strategies Report #1.* Boulder, CO.

The Beloit College Girls and Women in Science Project: Multiple Perspectives on Partnerships and Partnering

Kathleen Greene

Beloit College (Wisconsin)

Introduction

The Girls and Women in Science Project has several components involving persons from a number of communities. It connects Beloit College in partnership with the School District of Beloit and other Wisconsin and Illinois districts. The first section of this chapter consists of a brief history and description of the project's major components. The second section explores some of the significant partnerships this project represents. Then, the focus of the discussion shifts from formal to informal partnership, using "close-up" examples that convey the nature of the project and taking a look at some of the persons who work together to make Girls and Women in Science successful.

The Girls and Women in Science Project: A Description

The Beloit College Girls and Women in Science Project is a nationally recognized, recently replicated, middle-school science and mathematics outreach program with multiple, overlapping components of teacher enhancement, student enrichment, and parent education. The United States, through the Department of Education's Eisenhower Mathematics and Science Education Program, as well as through the Directorate for Education and Human Resources of the National Science Foundation, has identified as a national priority the need to keep girls interested in the study of science and mathematics. In 1991, Beloit College initiated the Girls and Women in Science Project as a response to that need.

Girls and Women in Science, which has been supported for the past five years by Eisenhower Mathematics and Science Education Program grants, aims to promote the study of science among middle school girls and undergraduate women. Each project runs for an academic year, and has as its centerpiece a weekend conference for fifty middle-school girls, their teachers and their parents. Both during the conference and throughout the school year, this teacher enhancement and networking project promotes the use of investigative problem-solving in science education among the fifty participating teachers. The fifty sixth-grade girls who come to Beloit College for the conference spend a weekend of science (and fun) on the campus with fifty undergraduate women who are pursuing the sciences, social sciences, and teaching. Girls and Women in Science is also designed to provide the parents of the participating girls with encouragement, information, and science experiences. In addition, the project builds solidarity and enhances the professional identity of the women students who plan and staff the weekend conference, support each other in their pursuit of science and other professional careers, and serve as ambassadors of independent higher education for visitors to the conference and readers of media reports.

Girls and Women in Science demonstrates contributions as well as benefits when colleges form partnerships with multiple communities. These multiple communities include (a) the locale, whose teachers and professionals help plan and teach in the project; (b) one hundred fifty middle-school students, teachers and parents from Wisconsin and Illinois; and (c) the campus community, over one hundred of whose members (including two dozen faculty) contribute significantly in time, energy, and expertise to the weekend conference and year-long project. Through the collective efforts of everyone involved, Beloit College is transformed by this unique project that celebrates the opportunities, challenges, and rewards for women in science. The ongoing energy and success of the Girls and Women in Science Project can be seen in various ways, including continued funding, a growing demand for the program, and the enthusiasm and loyalty of the teachers, faculty and students who participate year after year.

Partnerships

The Girls and Women Project represents one aspect of an ongoing, official partnership between Beloit College and the School District of Beloit. Parallel but less structured partnerships connect other school districts in Wisconsin and Illinois with Beloit College, via the middle-school teachers and students who participate. Also, the project is in a legal and programmatic partnership with the U.S. Department of Education by virtue of the Dwight D. Eisenhower Mathematics and Science Education Program grants which have supported the project financially. These partnerships are essential to the success of the Girls and Women in Science Project.

Each year, as grant proposals are prepared for submission, the project director meets with members of the curriculum office of the School District of Beloit to build into the next year's project those issues and goals which are district priorities. Other outcomes of this deliberation are the development of local recruitment strategies and logistical considerations. A formal partnership between the school district and the college's Department of Education has been in place for the last several years. Girls and Women in Science has played a small but continuing role in this relationship which has included Beloit College student teachers being placed with cooperating district teachers, and district staff and faculty teaching Beloit College courses and participating in other college and department activities.

With respect to the Eisenhower grants, teacher enhancement has been the most significant component of the project, requiring a commitment between the project faculty and the group of approximately fifty middle-school teachers that the project serves each year. This partnership involves many different persons interacting in several different ways, with the shared and ultimate goal of improving students' science education. Beloit College faculty, with the help of Beloit College education and science students, and science educators from Wisconsin and elsewhere, lead workshops for the participating teachers during the conference. Beloit College science faculty and students design and staff science investigation stations where the middle-school girls work during the Conference. The college also contracts with district and area teachers to lead technology workshops for participating parents and teachers.

A Semantic Shift

Something important is missing from this discussion, however. It is limiting and incomplete to describe the Girls and Women in Science Project only in terms of partnerships, perhaps because a traditional notion of "partnership" may conjure up images of formal business or professional arrangements made for mutual gain. "Partnership" as it is used here is a positive example of the appropriation of an idea from the business world; persons and institutions committed to working together toward mutually beneficial objectives. Therefore, it is difficult to articulate what makes the use of this notion of "partnership" problematic in communicating why Girls and Women in Science works, when the *reason* it works is precisely that people and institutions work together!

Allow, then, the execution of a slight semantic shift from talk of "partnerships" to talk of "partners." When the focus is changed from the union (the partnership) to those who unite and are united (the partners) it becomes possible to describe more effectively the Girls and Women in Science Project and what gives it shape and power, its partners. Such a shift might also be viewed as a move from a structural perspective to one that is more cultural. The remainder of this chapter is devoted to a discussion of some of the partners in Girls and Women in Science, and how they contribute to the project's success.

Partners

A subtle but significant difference between a view of partnerships and partners is one of formality. While a partnership often refers to a formal arrangement, the notion of partners connotes something more fluid, spontaneous and personal. In school, for example, students choose partners for jumping rope, for going out to recess, for working on math problems. They choose seat partners on field trips, and, when multi-age groupings occur, older students may be asked to choose younger partners, and vice versa. This casual notion seems particularly appropriate when discussing the interactions that occur and the relationships that develop through participation in Girls and Women in Science.

The first set of partners which emerges involves the undergraduate women who meet every week with the Project Director to plan and then staff the conference. The majority of undergraduates either have majors in science or social science or are preparing to teach. Meeting regularly over a semester allows them to understand better what their peers are experiencing. The college students' solidarity in turn affects the sixth-grade girls who arrive on campus for the weekend Conference. The undergraduate women pair up with the girls, first in get-acquainted activities on Friday afternoon, at dinner, and, later, during a recreational period and giant "sleepover" party at the Sports Center. This casual but personal interaction promotes a closeness between the girls and the undergraduates who become their role models, while at the same time, reinforcing enduring, positive relationships among the undergraduates. Addresses are frequently exchanged at the end of the conference, and it is common for girls to begin corresponding with each other or with one of the undergraduates when they arrive back home.

On Saturday, the sixth-grade girls (working in pairs), several of the undergraduates, and a dozen of the college science faculty work together at investigation stations, offering a variation on the usual interactions among the college faculty and students. When later on Saturday the middle-school teachers visit their students at the stations to hear about the girls' investigations, the teachers have an opportunity to witness how the college faculty and students interact as senior and junior colleagues, respectively. The interaction of the college science faculty with the middle-school teachers is also valuable for the college faculty, who become more cognizant and appreciative of the challenges middle school teachers encounter as they are called on to teach as many as six classes each day with very little preparation time and assistance.

Each middle-school teacher is asked to "partner up" with two other teachers for a hands-on science investigation session on Friday afternoon. The project director and other science educators, including Beloit College pre-service teachers, collaboratively plan and lead this session in which the teachers pursue an open-ended investigation of an environmental simulation. Thus the model of teaching and learning provided in this and other conference sessions is one of casual yet essential partnership, within and across levels of expertise and formal status. This is neither coincidental nor surprising, as group work and collaboration characterize science education at Beloit.

At one of the Saturday teacher sessions, teachers are asked to share a favorite science teaching activity or idea with the assembled group of teachers and teacher educators. This, too, promotes a kind of partnership among the teachers, and the view that the teachers are professionals with valuable ideas to share with colleagues. At another of the teacher sessions, Beloit College faculty from several departments lead a panel discussion in which an environmental issue is considered across disciplines. Later, in follow-up small-group discussions, the teachers, teacher educators, and faculty panelists work together to brainstorm ideas for promoting interdisciplinary learning in the middle school classroom.

In a final example of rather non-conventional and inter-generational partnering, a Beloit College science student who is also a pre-service teacher travelled across southern Wisconsin to the classrooms of twenty of the participating teachers in May 1995, to interview them about their involvement in Girls and Women in Science, their experiences teaching environmental science, and their ideas for improving the project. The teachers were remarkably gracious to this student (as they have been to all of the pre-service teachers involved in the project), often arranging for him to meet with other teachers and school administrators as well. The middle-school personnel were eager and interested to hear about

25

the latest in science education at Beloit College, and the student realized his good fortune to be taken under the wing of the teachers, who, acting as professional role models, shared valuable inside knowledge about teaching middle-school science. From all reports, everyone felt the school visits were useful and informative, providing yet another example of how informal partnerships have contributed significantly to the mutual respect and appreciation across and among the various groups of persons involved in the Girls and Women in Science Project, and ultimately to its success.

Conclusion

The previous pages represent an attempt to give readers a sense of how, through multiple channels of informal as well as formal interaction, the Beloit College Girls and Women in Science Project promotes partnership between and among Beloit College students and faculty, as well as Wisconsin and Illinois middle-school teachers, students and administrators. At times, partners have emerged in relatively unlikely places, having successfully navigated their way around existing, "natural" boundaries and obstacles. Benefits from these various partnerships have accrued to all groups involved: at the College, in the schools, and in the larger community, often in unpredicted and perhaps unpredictable ways. The partnerships are complex, diverse, multi-faceted, and often quite fluid and interpersonal. As such, they represent teaching and learning at their best.

Relationships as a Foundation: Emerging Field Experiences Within Multiple College-School Partnerships

Samuel J. Hausfather, Mary E. Outlaw, Elizabeth L. Strehle

Berry College (Georgia)

The professional development school concept represents a fundamental change in teacher education that can impact the teaching of methods classes, interaction within college classrooms, supervision of students in the field, and relationships with classroom teachers (Zeichner, 1992). This chapter describes the restructuring of education courses at a small liberal arts college and the resulting impact on relationships within both college and school classrooms.

The restructuring of the college education program will first be described, with special attention to the revision and integration of field experiences into college coursework. The relationships of college faculty, classroom teachers, and preservice teachers will be shared in describing a work-in-process. A preliminary analysis reveals benefits to college students accruing from the close supervision and intense experiences, yet little movement toward larger school reform goals. The many questions that remain will be explicated as important markers on the road to providing quality field experiences for all teacher education students within schools committed to thoughtful reform using the model of the professional development schools.

Relationships with schools

Berry College is a 1600-student private liberal arts college located in northwest Georgia. The college is founded on the commitment of

Martha Berry to serve the needs of those who might otherwise not have the chance for an education. Berry College provides scholarships and an intensive work program to help support many first-generation college students. At the same time, the college serves a population of mostly white, middle-class students attracted to its academic reputation, small-school atmosphere, and beauty. Education forms the largest major at the college.

The field experience program has long comprised an important component of the teacher education program. As the School of Education began preparations for reaccreditation by the state and the National Council for Accreditation of Teacher Education (NCATE), the office of field experiences coordinated a reorganization of the field experience program to meet accreditation standards. Various criteria were considered as important in the modifications to be instituted. Changes impacted all students in early childhood, middle school, and secondary levels of teacher preparation. Students had to be exposed to a variety of field experiences including placements in diverse multicultural, rural, and suburban environments, and at a variety of grade levels within the grade range for which they were being certified. Placements had to involve supervision by both college personnel and classroom teachers. Finally, placements represented an understanding of the theoretical models of education reflected in the students' college coursework.

Supervision of students in the field appeared to be a major stumbling block. Working in a small college without graduate assistants, college professors provided all the supervision given in the field. Two core courses existing within each education program, a general curriculum course and a general methods course, were restructured to become field-based courses. Four major modifications were made to each course. The course time was changed to meet during an entire morning two days a week. The field experience time was blocked into the course time such that one day the course would meet on campus and the other day of each week the course time would be used for the field experience placements. Placements would be made at a limited number of schools so that the course professor could be on site during the field experience placement, available for supervision of students and consultation with classroom teachers. The course content was restructured according to clusters that were shared across program areas and that built upon the assignments completed during the field experiences (see Table 1).

To make it feasible for one professor to supervise his or her class on the alternate days in the field, all students had to be placed either in one school or in two nearby schools. This arrangement required multiple placements, using many cooperating teachers, in one site. The

Table 1. Course content clusters: Field-based courses

Curriculum Courses 1. Foundations and organization of curriculum 2. Development of observation and reflection skills 3. Writing lesson plans 4. Working with parents, volunteers, and paraprofessionals Methods Courses 1. Classroom management 2. Writing unit and lesson plans 3. Teaching strategies 4. Classroom evaluation techniques

decision was made to place students in pairs within each classroom placement, allowing for more intensive coverage within a school building. Pairing students with a student partner for their classroom placement allowed more opportunities for students to get feedback on their classroom behavior. Partners observed each other teaching and working in the classroom, thus enabling them to provide each other with a different perspective on their activities. Partners provided mutual support, aiding each other in planning as well as responding to the pressures of classroom life. Beyond supporting the program goals, pairing enabled preservice teachers to see the value of collegial reflection, in contrast to the emphasis on individuality that, according to Zeichner (1992), is so prevalent in schools.

Establishing professional development relationships with schools was a natural outcome of the proposed field experience changes. Discussions began with the surrounding two school districts, the first item of business being to identify schools with which to begin collaborating on the expanded field experience placements. We identified these schools by targeting those where we had already built relationships through ongoing placement of field experience students or through adjunct faculty relationships with the school's principal; where we felt a sense of sincere welcome to our field experience students; or where a diverse student body was represented. Six schools were chosen, involving a feeder elementary, middle, and high school within the city school district and similarly within the county school district.

Relationships with teachers

During the fall of 1993, the director of field experiences and college faculty involved in the site supervision began making presentations to teachers at each school site at the beginning of each semester. These presentations evolved during these three years as we implemented changes in our thinking and moved toward partnership relationships with classroom teachers.

The classroom teacher's role was critical to the success of field experiences. It was acknowledged that teachers are restricted by their realities of time, resources, and context in their work with field experience students. At the same time, teachers were asked to find time to talk to the students about their planning and lessons, and to share the thinking behind the decisions they make. Field experience students were allowed to teach at least three lessons, one to a small group, one to the whole class with their partner, and one alone to the whole class. Structures designed to promote conversation between preservice and classroom teachers have been added. We introduced a framework for understanding the developmental levels of preservice teachers based on their own history and experiences (Strehle, 1995). We discussed the developmental levels of the field-experience students, providing teachers with a framework for understanding the field experience students (see Table 2).

Under each developmental level were listed tasks preservice teachers may engage in during their time in the field. Supervising teachers were encouraged to add to or delete from the list, making it their own. We also presented a rubric for observations by teachers or fellow students that emphasizes the concepts covered in the college classroom and that allows for regular structured feedback by the classroom teacher (see Table 3).

Teachers are also encouraged to maintain a conversation notebook with their field experience students where questions, concerns, and notes may be written by teacher or student, allowing for questioning and responding to concerns within the busy schedules. We closed our meetings by looking to the future, with the hope that closer communication between the college and the school would provide an opening for collaboration between practicing teachers and college professors. The desire and need to learn from each other was emphasized as we shared a glimpse of the professional development school vision. Field experience students were then introduced and met with their supervising teacher to introduce themselves and see the classroom for the first time.

Following prearranged schedules, college faculty and students were on site approximately one full morning a week. College faculty made the rounds, visiting classrooms and observing both preservice teachers and the regular goings-on in the classroom. Conversations over practice and the concerns of preservice and inservice teachers occurred after observations, in hallways and classrooms, and through journals.

Reflection by the field experience student was emphasized through daily journal entries focusing on analysis of significant episodes (Posner,

Table 2: Developmental Flow of Field Experience

OBSERVER: Building a relationship with the supervising teacher Watching teacher
*observing lessons taught*observing classroom management*observing students
Completing clerical tasks
*grading papers Directing routine activities
*calendar Completing college assignments
*making seating charts*writing notes for journals*interviewing students*questionnaire
PARTICIPANT-OBSERVER: Developing relationships with students Assisting individual students
*helping with seat work*one on one reading*conference with student writing*assisting student with make up work
Teaching lessons in small groups
*implementing lesson plans
CO-PARTICIPANT: Matching supervising teacher's classroom management
Exploring individual concept of teaching
Sharing classroom responsibilities
*plan and teach lesson to class*lead discussion of current events*implementing classroom management*accompany on a field trip
Adapted from Strehle, 1995

1993). Field experience students were encouraged to move reflection beyond merely the technical level. Through classroom discussion and written responses to their journal entries, college faculty emphasized three levels of reflection (Adler, 1990):

> Technical Rationality—reflections on WHAT happened; focuses on events relying on personal experience and/or observations without regard for a system or theory (Cruikshank, 1987); Practical Action or Contextual—reflections on WHY decisions were made; concerned with clarifying the assumptions and predispositions underlying competing pedagogical goals and with assessing the educational consequences toward which a teaching action leads (Schon, 1983, 1987); Ethical or Critical Reflection—reflections on what SHOULD be; concerned with the worth of knowledge and the social circumstances useful to students (Van Manen, 1977; Zeichner & Liston, 1987).

Table 3: Rubric for co-participation in field experience lesson

Lesson planning Pre-conference with cooperating teacher concerning content of lesson planned.
plan approved Lesson Implementation Setting Stage:
use of prior knowledge/review
Content:
appropriateness use of visuals connection to previously learned material abstract concept made concrete/concrete made abstract
Relationship to students:
use of oral language proximity behavior (management) techniques learning strategy used to engage students in learning involvement of all students
Closure:
connect to specific content areas
(if appropriate)review of concept introduced/reviewed
Comments/Feedback:
Relationships as a foundation:
Emerging field experiences within multiple college-school partnerships

The college classroom became the location of an essential dialogue between preservice teacher and college professor. Both were active participants in this conversation which was designed to yield understanding of practice. We were able to take advantage of an important developmental time in the construction of preservice teachers—concepts of education—a trying-out time in which preservice teachers tested and reflected on what education is and can be, in which theory and practice intersected. Whereas student teaching is more oriented toward testing and reflecting on student teachers—identity as a teacher and their role in ethical, contextual, and power issues, early field experiences provide a formative time of even greater need for ongoing supervision, guidance, and guided reflection on experience.

Tomorrow's Schools (The Holmes Group, 1990) confirmed that teachers are one of teacher education's biggest untapped resources. Teachers, however, have been quick to point out that the realities of classroom conditions do not allow for quality mentoring or reflection time. Therefore we decided to set aside time when classroom teachers and college faculty could step back from the process and reflect on what we had learned and where we were going. In the spring of each year, a full-day retreat has been held for classroom teachers, school administrators, and college faculty committed to collaboration between the college and evolving professional development schools.

The retreat has focused on supervisory techniques, curricular dialogue, and program refinement. Its goals have been to plan for sustaining the field-based relationships, to share appropriate supervisory techniques, and to begin the design of a continuing relationship. Groups have discussed the goals and expectations involved in the field experiences accompanying specific teacher education courses. There has been much discussion and delineation of suggestions for improvements in the field-experience assignments, with a list generated of specific suggestions for improvements. These have included such areas as how much assistance or guidance students should be given, concern about accuracy and sharing of journal entries, planning time and procedures, teacher expectations, and the role of preservice students in classroom management. Time to mentor and reflect continues to pose a significant problem without an easy answer within the classroom context. Teachers have expressed the desire for more support and sharing, both with college faculty and with school faculty at other sites. Participants have expressed interest in increased collaboration in the future to create new roles for school and college faculty.

The retreat has provided an opportunity to emphasize the importance of building relationships between the college and the involved schools. A clear sense of direction has been developed, along with a core group of committed staff at each of our field-based sites. This core group expresses a clear appreciation for the teacher education process and the supervision of field-experience students. More important, they have become colleagues with whom we can continue the conversation. The retreat provides an excellent basis for the long-term relationships necessary between school and college practitioners. It begins with this person-to-person communication between school and college faculty which facilitates our working together to achieve the short- and long-term goals we have together delineated.

Preservice teachers building relationships in schools

> Connie sits cross-legged on the sidewalk outside the kindergarten classroom carefully stuffing straw into the body of a scarecrow. The five-year-olds beside her take the straw from the ground and carefully place it between the buttons of the scarecrow's blue plaid shirt. Inside the classroom, Jennifer asks questions about baby animals to a group of children clustered around the book center. At the far end of the room three students seated at a small table cut out farm animals and match them to their mother. The cooperating teacher and

aide are at the back of the classroom pouring juice for the afternoon snack.

The field experience offers an opportunity for preservice teachers to practice teaching through designing lessons and working with children. The teacher education program is complex with the core of the education courses concentrated in the junior year. The curriculum class is the beginning of the focus of the junior year block; it enables preservice teachers to begin examining the practice of teaching in the context of their field experience. The college instructor has the task of designing the class to meet the individual needs of the students as well as to support their field experience by observing them, providing written feedback, and offering an opportunity for reflection. The field experience is an integral part of the dynamic process of giving students an opportunity to integrate their understanding of teaching and to discuss their practice with a professional educator. The pre-service teachers find their field experience an opportunity to put into action the lessons they plan. The classroom always adds a dimension of problem solving the preservice teachers have not had the opportunity to explore until this time.

Conversation among the preservice teachers extends to discussions concerning how to implement the tasks in the lessons they are assigned to teach in their college classes. In the pre-kindergarten class of four-year-olds, Marilyn and Ellen are always wondering how to implement literacy tasks into a preschool curriculum that does not emphasize the reading and writing connection. Through conversations with their supervising teacher and college instructors, Marilyn and Ellen are able to design literacy activities that would meet the needs of the four-year-olds in their pre-kindergarten classroom. The result: a group of four-year-olds huddle around Marilyn and listen to a story about bears. After listening for a moment or two, one student gets up, goes to the book shelf, and selects her own book. She begins to read to herself, making up the story as she goes along.

Preservice teachers who teach lessons together in the context of a small group are given the opportunity to learn about collaborative teaching. Ellen and Linda, best friends and roommates, showed tremendous growth in planning lessons and working with students as they continually talked about teaching through two semesters of working together in a field experience. After gaining confidence by presenting discovery lessons in small groups, they began to implement discovery lessons in large groups when they taught in a fifth grade classroom the following semester. Working in pairs the pre-service teachers had the opportunity to generate ideas, plan lessons together, and begin to think of teaching as connecting lessons to the students. As a result: the third graders gather around a small table and listen to instructions from Ellen and Linda. Gently the children place their hands into a pan of sticky-gloopy-green slime. They move their hands across the bottom of the pan and then lift them up. There is no end to discovering all the different ways to make the slime go. Slime runs down hands onto the table and eventually onto the floor. After a quick trip to the bathroom one little girl rushes through the door and heads toward Ellen. "What is the recipe for that slime? I want to show my mom."

The relationships that develop between the preservice teacher and the classroom teacher are the beginning of an ongoing dialogue about students and teaching. The opportunities to see teaching in a positive light are often left up to the classroom teacher, and teachers who value the education of future teachers enthusiastically share their classrooms. The college instructor provides instructional time to help the student make connections between the theoretical concepts and the manifestation of these concepts in the classroom of the cooperating teacher. This type of instruction presents teaching as a problem-solving process giving preservice teachers an opportunity to see teaching as a decision-making process based on their own beliefs about teaching.

Conversations about teaching are vital during field-based classes (Hollingsworth, 1992). The conversation with the college instructor provides opportunities to connect what is learned in the classroom with what is being learned in the field experience. The conversation with the cooperating teacher provides a framework for reflection on the curriculum and the students that a college classroom discussion does not offer. The contribution a classroom teacher makes in the development of the preservice teacher impacts the pre-service teacher's understanding of teaching. In Connie's case, the cooperating teacher was concerned that Connie did not share many of her teaching ideas while paired with Jennifer, a more aggressive partner when it came to initiating instruction. Through ongoing observation and conversations about Connie with the college supervisor, the cooperating teacher stated that Connie, though not a strong initiator of her ideas, participated effectively in the development and implementation of lessons developed for the thematic unit. The time the cooperating teacher spent with Connie and Jennifer in giving feedback from the lesson planning and lesson implementation were opportunities for Connie and Jennifer to begin to reflect on their own teaching. Through these experiences Connie and Jennifer were given opportunities to consider how they could work together more effectively. Concern for Connie's feelings about her participation in sharing lessons with Jennifer extended to a dialogue between her college instructors and cooperating teacher where they shared their own observation about her growth. Connie left her field placement confident of her contribution in planning and working with kindergarten students. When preservice students are given ongoing feedback that supports their growth, they gain confidence and become eager to talk about their teaching with another professional.

Preservice teachers enter the field with a focus on providing educational opportunities that are developmentally appropriate for the students in their classrooms. This practice extends into knowing and understanding the social, physical, and psychological development of students and striving to develop a curriculum that invites students to learn. Learning through active involvement is a goal that preservice teachers provide for their students in classrooms that many times are not set up for this method of learning. The classrooms in which preservice teachers are placed do not always reflect the theories that the students teachers are learning about in their college classrooms. Rich conversations exist when students enter the field and find that their understanding of teaching is not necessarily what they see in their practicum. When the preservice teachers describe their relationship with their supervising teacher they say such things as, "I like her as a person but did not agree with a lot of her teaching methods," and "I saw things that I don't want to, which was good, but I didn't see things I wish that I had." The conversations exist when students are supported and encouraged to reflect on the issues in the classrooms and to reflect on how they feel the classrooms could be.

The preservice teachers are given the opportunity to think about their own practice and what choices they have teaching in the classroom of their cooperating teacher. Preservice teachers are asked to reflect and articulate their own beliefs about practice. College faculty have observed preservice teachers maturing in personal and professional behaviors and decision making abilities. The worth of the effort is evident in the remarks of a student regarding the benefits derived from early field-based experiences: "comfort and confidence in my teaching ability, a greater enthusiasm for 'getting out there,' going into new situations with different students with a more positive 'can do' attitude, a greater desire to help bring about change, improvement and progressivism in the field of education, improved interpersonal skills—dealing with a variety of students/building relationships with professionals, peers, and superiors, and a much greater knowledge base/resource base upon which I will construct my philosophy as an educator!"

Evolving relationships: Preliminary evaluations

The program has been in place for two years, with students from the first field-based courses now having completed student teaching. Implementation of the field experience has been monitored through direct observation by college faculty, questionnaires completed by students and teachers, informal conversations with teachers and students, faculty presentations in schools, planned retreats for college and school faculty, and evaluations completed by student teachers. Throughout this time period various modifications have been instituted on the basis of continuing feedback and discussions among college faculty, students and school faculties.

Initial dialogue with the teachers showed immediate concern for having time to devote to mentoring our college students. Teachers were quick to point out that the realities of classroom conditions did not allow for quality mentoring time. During the semesters of implementation, discussion of the time issue has continued and adjustments have been initiated in an attempt to address the concern. For example, in spring 1995 students were assigned five hours as "free" hours to be scheduled outside of the regular morning time block. This designation provided time for meeting during the teacher's planning period, or after school, and also gave the student credit for the additional time. Many students and teachers had already chosen to meet at other times in order to plan lessons and to discuss the complexities of the specific classroom. Each semester the authors observed teachers taking more ownership in the process of educating preservice teachers and finding the time needed for effective mentoring.

Observations by teachers of student performance during the field experience proved to be insightful and supportive of the goals of the program. One teacher commented that she "did observe quite a bit of personal growth in both students. As the semester progressed there was improvement in presentations and in relating to the needs of the students." Another teacher observed that the students "are still growing and learning about being a teacher." The students also reflected on the experience. One stated, "I've been able to see some ideas I have had work and flop. Sometimes the ideas floating around in my head seem great, but when I implement them all types of questions come up. This gives me the chance to think about things I wouldn't normally think about."

The use of student pairs has been helpful in most cases. Student reports on working in pairs included the following comments:

> Was wonderful—lots of support and encouragement, bounced
> plan ideas off each other; I did not get much feedback from the

> classroom teacher, so it really helped to have someone there to bounce ideas off of and to give me suggestions;
>
> Always had someone to fall back on; Very helpful—relieves a lot of stress; and Like the moral support.

Teachers noticed the positive aspects as well, including statements such as,

> they seem to feel more comfortable working together; This was great for them and for me. Working together really helped boost their confidence level and made the experience much less intimidating; and the two pooled their strengths and talents. They seemed to feel less threatened.

On occasion, student pairs have had difficulty. Working together over an extended period requires interpersonal skills that some students have not had the opportunity to develop.

Effective communication among all parties is an on-going process in which we are all engaged. During the first year some teachers noted that they "never had time to talk to the college instructor," and that "It was more difficult to communicate with professors than students though the communication was somewhat better than in other similar experiences." Another teacher wrote, "Since the guidelines were clearly stated, little communication was really necessary." The college faculty saw the need for improved communication when a teacher complained, "I think too many assignments were given to the Berry students. I don't mind having practicum students, but it took too much of my teaching time." The benefit many teachers derive from participation in the field experience is the additional teaching assistance the practicum students provide.

Graduates of Berry who completed the first cycle of early field experiences in the field based courses and who have recently completed student teaching rated the experiences highly on the Student Evaluation of the Teacher Education Program. In response to the question "What aspects of the Education Program at Berry College were most helpful in preparation for your perceived career?" graduates made comments like the following:

- "All the practice experiences and field experiences,"

- "The practicums were the most helpful, because we put into practice what we learned,"

- "The number of field experiences linked to course work" (16 others mentioned this),

- "Field experiences, student teaching, student working at the elementary school,"

- "The field experiences combined with reflection journals and excellent courses."

Time and opportunities for communication seem to be the major challenges for continued progress in effectively collaborating for the benefit of both classroom teachers and our preservice teachers. This is not unusual within professional development school efforts. Creating a climate of open communication and facilitating that communication are seen as key aspects of many professional development efforts (Robinson & Darling-Hammond, 1994). Given the different cultures, roles, and status between colleges and schools, misunderstandings are inevitable. Recognizing and accommodating these differences involves increased personal open communication (Green, Baldini, & Stack, 1993).

Discussion

The relationships between the college faculty and cooperating teachers have resulted in a desire to empower the classroom teacher to share in the responsibility of educating the preservice teachers. This task begins by sharing the responsibility of supervision with the classroom teacher. As the cooperating teachers engage in conversations with the preservice teacher, they contemplate theoretical implications as well as practical issues involved in teaching. Our greatest challenge is to rethink the role of the classroom teacher as an equal partner in the teacher education effort. Through an emphasis on relationships, we see connections with schools as an essential component of our college teaching. An effort to link the college methods classes to the field experience is accomplished through observations of the preservice teachers, reading their reflective journals and responding to feedback from the cooperating teachers. The understanding gained allow the college faculty to integrate issues of common concern into the college classroom.

Bringing teachers in as equal partners is problematic. Given the different cultures of school and college, misunderstandings are inevitable (Green, Baldini, & Stack, 1993). Preconceived concepts of role and status difference can lead to hesitation and difficulties in collaboration. These individual differences must be recognized and accommodated in order to develop relationships with schools. Colleges cannot impose their own agenda on schools, an approach found to be ineffective in promoting change (MacNaughton & Johns, 1993). Professional development schools must be cultivated through a collaborative effort at seeking solutions to commonly defined problems. Collaboration involves equality, balance, and cooperative relationships (Hall, 1993). It is a long and time-consuming process that cannot be rushed! If change is to be longstanding, it must result from a developing coherence in perspectives between school and college faculty (Stoddart, 1993). This will take time, energy, and commitment.

The college faculty is committed to the goal of incorporating professional development school relationships into our teacher education program. Building relationships with the supervising teachers is a journey that is time-consuming and developmental. The degree to which we can be effective is based on the level of involvement of college faculty and the interest of school faculty. Our goal has been to serve all students in the school of education. We have made significant progress with our elementary education model, but have much further to go with our secondary model. Only through dedication and hard work does change happen. Developing relationships takes time. Sustaining relationships takes time. Just to make time to listen to each other is progress.

Our goal is to carefully place preservice teachers with caring professionals with whom they will be able to begin to reflect on their own understanding of what it is to be a teacher. As college faculty and classroom teachers get to know each other and become partners, there is potential for a better environment for understanding teaching for preservice teachers, supervising teachers, and college faculty.

References

Adler, S. A. (1990). The reflective practitioner and the curriculum of teacher education. Paper presented at the annual meeting of the Association of Teacher Educators, Las Vegas.

Cruikshank, D. R. (1987). *Reflective teaching: The preparation of students of teaching*. Reston, VA: Association of Teacher Educators.

Green, N., Baldini, B., & Stack, W. M. (1993). Spanning cultures: Teachers and professors in professional development schools. *Action in Teacher Education, 15(2)*, 18-24.

Hall, J. L. (1993). Perception of collaborative partners in a professional development school project. *Contemporary Education, 64*, 239-242.

Hollingsworth, S. (1992). Learning to teach through collaborative conversation: A feminist approach. *American Educational Research Journal, 29*, 373-404.

Holmes Group. (1990). *Tomorrow's schools: Principles of the design of professional development schools*. East Lansing, MI: Author.

MacNaughton, R. H., & Johns, F. (1993). The professional development school: An emerging concept. *Contemporary Education, 64*, 215-218.

Posner, G. J. (1993). *Field experience: A guide to reflective teaching* (3rd edition). New York: Longman.

Robinson, S. P., & Darling-Hammond, L. (1994). Change for collaboration and collaboration for change: Transforming teaching through school-university partnerships. In L. Darling-Hammond (Ed.), *Professional development schools: Schools for developing a profession*. New York: Teachers College Press.

Schon, D. A. (1983). *The reflective practitioner: How professionals think in action*. New York: Basic Books.

Schon, D. A. (1987). *Educating the reflective practitioner: Toward a new design for teaching and learning in the professions*. San Francisco: Jossey-Bass.

Strehle, E. L. (1995). *Negotiating uncertainty: Making sense of the student teaching experience*. Unpublished doctoral dissertation, Virginia Polytechnic Institute and State University.

Stoddart, T. (1993). *The professional development school: Building bridges between cultures*. Educational Policy, 7, 5-23.

Van Manen, M. (1977). Linking ways of knowing with ways of being practical. *Curriculum Inquiry, 6,* 205-228.

Zeichner, K. (1992). Rethinking the practicum in the professional development school partnership. *Journal of Teacher Education, 43,* 296-307.

Zeichner, K. M. & Liston, D. P. (1987). Teaching student teachers to reflect. *Harvard Educational Review, 57,* 23-48.

Foxfire: Lighting the Way for Collaboration in Teacher Education

Sharon T. Teets
Ronald G. Midkiff

Carson-Newman College (Tennessee)

In what Ann Lieberman has referred to as the "second wave of educational reform" (1988, p. vii), college/university and school partnerships are viewed as essential to the teacher education process (Sirotnik & Goodlad, 1988; Guest, 1993). Faculty and administrators in teacher education units are searching for effective ways to build collaborative relationships with practitioners so that partnerships are effective for both the improvement of teacher education programs and P-12 schools. Because many collaborations evolve informally and idiosyncratically based on individual faculty members' involvement in P-12 schools, the resulting formalized relationships are either strengthened or flawed by the processes and attitudes involved in the development of the relationships (Darling-Hammond, 1994; Goodlad, 1994; Holmes Group, 1990; Simpson, 1994; Teitel, 1994).

This chapter is structured to illustrate how the developmental process involved in collaborating with P-12 teachers has significantly affected the effectiveness and potential for future development of a more formal partnership relationship as defined in the professional literature (Goodlad, 1988; 1994). Specifically, the article includes a description of how Carson-Newman College began its collaboration with the Foxfire Fund, Inc. and P-12 teachers, an overview of the Foxfire approach, and how the approach itself has served as the driving force behind the collaboration.

How did the collaboration begin?

The collaboration is rooted in Carson-Newman's strategic planning process in which existing strengths were identified, one of which was that of faculty interest and expertise in the area of Appalachian Studies. In order to maximize this strength, the College established a Center for Educational Service to Appalachia (CESA). The Center was designed to showcase faculty, student, and regional artists/writers' work and to serve as a resource for the broader community of individuals who would not necessarily enroll in traditional college classes. A first activity of the Center was to establish an annual award for an individual or group who had provided exemplary educational service to the region. The award recipient was featured as a guest lecturer to campus, public school, and other community groups.

The first recipient of the CESA award was Eliot Wigginton, high school English teacher and editor of the well-known student-produced *Foxfire* book series, which documents Appalachian traditions in photography and text. Public school teachers responded enthusiastically to the presentations and expressed interest in learning more about the use of the Foxfire approach. Serendipitously, the Appalachian Regional Commission awarded the Foxfire Fund, Inc., a grant to establish a Foxfire training center and teacher network in Tennessee, and the Foxfire program was established through the Graduate Studies Department in the Division of Education in 1989. Since that time, over 300 teachers have participated in training to use the approach in their classrooms, and the East Tennessee Teachers Network was formed to provide ongoing training and support for the use of Foxfire in Tennessee's schools. In order to understand how the network and teacher educators collaborate, a review of the approach itself is essential, for it is the approach that forms the driving force for the collaboration.

What is Foxfire?

The Foxfire approach to teaching began in 1966 in a high school English class in Rabun County, Georgia, when the teacher encountered repeated failures to involve students in meaningful learning activities. The teacher and students finally launched a magazine, named *Foxfire*, which was edited and expanded into the popular Foxfire book series (Wigginton, 1985). Initial efforts to replicate the Foxfire success resulted in some 200 short-lived magazine projects, and it was not until 20 years after the founding of Foxfire, that training to "do Foxfire" focused not on magazines and books, but rather on the approach to teaching used in the process of producing the successful magazine and book series. The organization now identifies as its mission:

> . . . to teach, model, and refine an active, learner-centered
> approach to education which is academically sound and pro-
> motes continuous interaction between students and their com-
> munities, so that students will find fulfillment as creative,
> productive, critical citizens. (*What is Foxfire?*, n.d., p. 2)

The approach is used across the nation by teachers of students from preschool through the college years, in almost all curricular areas. In order to articulate the essential elements of the Foxfire approach more clearly, a list of core practices was devised, based on the reflections of students and teachers on the qualities of good teachers and memorable learning activities from their own past educational experiences (*Foxfire*, 1990):

1. All the work teachers and students do together must flow from student desire, student concerns.

2. The role of the teacher must be that of collaborator and team leader and guide, rather than boss.

3. The academic integrity of the work must be absolutely clear.

4. The work is characterized by student action.

5. A constant feature of the process is its emphasis on peer teaching, small group work, and team work.

6. Connections between the classroom and surrounding communities and the real world outside the classroom are clear.

7. There must be an audience beyond the teacher for student work.

8. As the year progresses, new activities should spiral gracefully out of the old, incorporating lessons learned from past experiences, building on skills and understanding that can now be amplified.

9. As teachers, we must acknowledge the worth of aesthetic experience.

10. Reflection—some conscious, thoughtful time to stand apart from the work itself—is an essential activity that must take place at key points throughout the work.

11. The work must include unstintingly honest, ongoing evaluation for skills and content, and changes in student attitude.

Teachers who implement the approach do so in a variety of ways, but they usually begin simply by comparing their own practice against the core practices, gradually incorporating more of each of the core practices into their own work with students. Many teachers use Foxfire to plan projects—they begin by sharing the academic goals and objectives with students, brainstorming with students where this knowledge, attitude, or skill is used in the world beyond the classroom. The students and teacher brainstorm "real world" projects that might be done to incorporate the knowledge, attitudes, or skills to be mastered. At all stages of the project, students are involved actively in planning, implementing, and evaluating their work. Teachers and students, together, work toward incorporating as many of the core practices as possible into each project. Together, they raise questions such as, "How are we going to know that we have mastered the content through this project? Who will be the audience for our work? In what ways will we involve the community? What have we learned so far? and What do we need to do next?"

How is the Foxfire training collaborative?

Although initial Foxfire training occurs within the context of a three-hour graduate course at Carson-Newman College, Foxfire training occurs in a variety of formats throughout the country. As Foxfire course facilitators have gained more experience in training teachers to use the approach, a number of "givens" for the course have developed. The most critical element of each Foxfire course is that the approach must be modeled for teachers. It is not enough to train teachers, for example, in strategies to work with students in groups; teachers must experience learning about the approach through the use of group work. It is not enough to "tell" teachers that they need to base instruction on student experience; the teachers' experiential base must be the starting point for discussion. In order to help teachers construct their own views of good teaching, the initial introduction to the course requires teachers to reflect upon their own learning experiences, as well as the experiences they provide for the students they teach. After the core practices are discussed in relationship to their own experiences, teachers are actively involved in setting the agenda for the course. Just as teachers are expected to involve their students in planning instruction, the question is posed to the teachers in the course, "How shall we structure the course so that you will feel confident about trying to implement this approach when you go back to your classroom?"

Because participants in Foxfire courses are usually teaching in P-12 settings, a second given of a Foxfire course is that P-12 classroom teachers who have been implementing the approach must be part of the instructional team. First- or second-year implementers of the approach serve as guests for the Foxfire course. As they become more experienced in the use of the approach, and as they learn more about teaching the adult learner, classroom teachers serve as co-instructors for the course.

A third given in Foxfire training is that the introductory course is only the beginning. Based on past experience with teachers using the approach, as well as the recommendations of literature related to the adoption of educational innovation (Joyce & Showers, 1980; Boyd, 1994)), follow-up services are provided through the East Tennessee Teachers Network. Teachers participate in meetings which focus primarily on sharing ideas with other teachers; course facilitators may visit the teachers' classrooms; teachers may visit experienced Foxfire teachers' classrooms; and they may participate in additional Foxfire training offered either regionally or nationally by the Foxfire Fund, Inc.

The network, coordinated by a Carson-Newman faculty member and a P-12 teacher experienced in the use of the Foxfire approach, is led by the teachers. A steering committee governs the program and activities of the network. For example, in response to teacher and administrator concerns about the impact of the Foxfire approach on standardized achievement test scores, a grant was secured to provide training in alternative forms of assessment, as well as to document student progress on standardized test measures (Teets, 1990; Hange, 1992). Also in response to teachers' requests, a second-level Foxfire course was developed, and an emphasis area within the existing Master's program was created for teachers who are interested in deepening their understanding of the approach. In addition to planning and presenting their work at network meetings, teachers are provided with other professional development opportunities through publishing or presenting their work at professional meetings (Duncan, Teets, & Turnbull, 1993; Mobley & Teets, 1992; Teets, Dittmer, Dollar, Midkiff, & Turnbull, 1993). The network also has published its work in and served as guest editors for the Foxfire journal, *Hands On*.

What other collaborations have developed?

The Foxfire training program has resulted in additional college/school collaborations. One of the first outgrowths of the network was that teacher education students were placed in Foxfire-trained teachers' classrooms for practicum and student-teaching experiences. A second outgrowth has been the inclusion of Foxfire teachers as guest lecturers and as course instructors in teacher education classes on campus. Additionally, Foxfire-trained teachers are serving on the policy making bodies of the Teacher Education Department, largely due to network teachers' interest in the inclusion of Foxfire training in the undergraduate teacher education program. Discussions are ongoing to incorporate the Foxfire approach as the model of instruction in a potential professional development school site, with the teacher education faculty and the public school faculty being trained to use the Foxfire approach in their classrooms.

The network has served to facilitate the collaboration of P-12 teachers with college faculty members in other academic departments. Initial guest appearances as content resource persons often lead to further collaborations, particularly for finding funding for projects of mutual interest. For example, the director of the Center for Educational Service to Appalachia, was initially introduced to teachers as a guest speaker in the Foxfire classes. He now frequently serves as a guest in P-12 classrooms where he shares his own poetry and also brings other resource persons who are presenters on the college campus through CESA to public school classrooms. In the past year, he and one of the teachers, along with her third grade children, acquired funding from the Tennessee Humanities Council to study the effects of the Tennessee Valley Authority on the people of the region.

As evidence of the teachers' embracing the core practice on spiraling, as well as the core practices on collaboration and community, other cooperative projects have developed among Foxfire-trained teachers and students that are not directly related to the teacher education program. For example, when one teacher and her students chose to use photography in meeting language arts objectives, contacts with community resources resulted in photography demonstrations by various professionals and donations of equipment and materials for the students to use. Teachers in the network represent significant resources for each other. Teacher-initiated collaborations, both with each other and with others outside P-12 schools, do eventually affect Carson-Newman's teacher education program, because they provide wonderful models for teacher education students who do practicum experiences and student teaching in their classrooms. A second kind of indirect collaboration has resulted in more communication across grade levels. Because P-12 teachers are enrolled in the same course, an opportunity is provided for elementary and secondary teachers to communicate with each other about various issues that affect schools. In addition, because of the core practice on audience, several teachers and students have chosen other classrooms within their own schools as the audience for their work. The communication between teachers and students of differing grade levels has opened numerous opportunities for peer teaching and modeling for students and additional opportunities for teachers to discuss the teaching-learning process. All of these cooperative ventures help teachers to refine their skills for problem-solving and collaboration.

Summary

Collaboration between colleges/university and P-12 schools is clearly desirable; yet, many barriers exist to prevent the formation of partnership relationships. Although the collaboration between Carson-Newman College and P-12 teachers is certainly not a partnership as formally defined by Goodlad (1988), the collaboration contains elements that may ensure success as future plans are made:

1. The collaboration began as a part of the overall college mission and received support from several different departments as well as the central administration;

2. The skills necessary for collaborating are modeled and directly taught through the Foxfire course itself; therefore, any teachers and college faculty members entering into collaborative ventures have a common frame of reference for solving potential problems; and

3. While the initial Foxfire program was established with external funding, the program has now become institutionalized within the existing graduate program. Both P-12 teachers and college faculty and administrators recognize the need for ongoing support for teachers and faculty to develop as true partners in training teachers.

In a time of rapid change in the field of teacher education, the potential for maximizing the existing collaboration for future development hinges upon multiple factors. However, the continued commitment of both teachers and the college community to an approach to teaching, which itself is a model for adaptation to change, is certainly a strength. Reflection, one of the most important core practices of the approach, will be vitally important as new directions are charted for the future. As Mary Catherine Bateson has said,

> Men and women confronting change are never fully prepared for the demands of the moment, but they are strengthened to meet uncertainty if they can claim a history of improvisation and a habit of reflection. (Bateson, 1994, p. 6)

Notes

1. Funding for the Foxfire program has been provided by the Appalachian Regional Commission, Carson-Newman College, Foxfire Fund, Inc., and the Lyndhurst Foundation.

2. Eliot Wigginton is no longer with the Foxfire Fund, Inc.

References

Bateson, M. C. (1994). *Peripheral visions: Learning along the way*. New York: HarperCollins Publishers.

Boyd, P. C. (1994). Professional school reform and public school renewal: Portrait of a partnership. *Journal of Teacher Education, 45* (2), 132-139.

Darling-Hammond, L. (Ed.). (1994). *Professional development schools: Schools for developing a profession*. New York: Teachers College Press.

Duncan, B., Teets, S.T., & Turnbull, D. (1993). Issues and strategies of assessment in student-centered classrooms. Discussion session presented at the annual meeting of the American Educational Research Association. Atlanta, Georgia.

Foxfire Fund, Inc. (n.d.) *What is Foxfire?* Mountain City, GA.

Goodlad, J. (1994). *Education renewal: Better teachers, better schools*. San Francisco: Jossey-Bass.

Goodlad, J. I. (1988). School-university partnerships for educational renewal: Rationale and concepts. In K. A. Sirotnik & J. I. Goodlad (Eds.), *School-university partnerships in action: Concepts, cases, and concerns* (pp. 3-31). New York: Teachers College Press.

Guest, L. S. (1993). *Improving teacher preparation: What the reform reports recommend*. Denver: Education Commission of the States.

Hange, J. E. (1992). Fostering change through college-school collaborative minigrants. Paper presented at the annual meeting of the American Association of Colleges for Teacher Education, San Antonio, TX. (ERIC Document Reproduction Service No. ED 350 251)

Holmes Group. (1990). *Tomorrow's schools: Principles for the design of professional development schools*. East Lansing, MI: Author.

Joyce, B., & Showers, B. (1980). Improving inservice training: The messages of research. *Educational Leadership, 37*, 379-385.

Lasley, J. (1992). Education's "impossible dream:" Collaboration. *Teacher Education and Practice, 7* (2), 17-22.

Lieberman, A. (Ed.) (1988). *Building a professional culture in schools*. New York: Teachers College Press.

Mobley, J., & Teets, S.T. (1992). "Informal assessment in second grade: A Foxfire story." In C. Genishi (Ed.), *Ways of assessing children and curriculum: Stories of early childhood practice* (pp. 163-190). New York: Teachers College Press.

Simpson, D. J. (1994). "Professional development schools, prescriptions and proscriptions: A fictitious letter to Evangelina Ramirez." *Journal of Teacher Education, 45* (4), 253-260.

Sirotnik, K. A., & Goodlad, J. I. (Eds.). 1988. *School-university partnership in action: Concepts, cases, and concerns*. New York: Teachers College Press.

Teets, S.T. (1990, November). The Foxfire approach and alternative forms of assessment: A comparison with student performance on standardized tests. Minigrant Research Report submitted to the Appalachian Educational Laboratory.

Teets, S.T., Dittmer, A., Dollar, A., Midkiff, R., & Turnbull, D. (1993, February). "The Foxfire approach to teaching: Shining moments in the collaborations of teachers and teacher educators." Symposium session presented at the annual meeting of the American Association of Colleges for Teacher Education. San Diego, California.

Teitel, L. (1994). "Can school-university partnerships lead to the simultaneous renewal of schools and teacher education?" *Journal of Teacher Education*, *45* (4), 245-252).

Wigginton, B.E. (1985). *Sometimes a shining moment.* New York: Doubleday.

A Collaborative Program to Train And Certify Bilingual Teachers

Diane A. Guay

College of Notre Dame (California)

Introduction

Like many teacher education programs housed in small, private colleges, we found it difficult to recruit students from under-represented groups because of one reason: cost. The cost factor keeps many talented bilingual students from applying. Yet, the location of our college, about 25 miles south of San Francisco, and the fact that it houses the only teacher education program in San Mateo County, makes us an ideal choice for many teacher candidates. Further, because we have student teaching contracts with 36 school districts, covering a wide area from South San Francisco to the coast and from the central peninsula to Silicon Valley, our students have wonderful opportunities for professional preparation as teachers.

As a fifth year (graduate) program, we have little scholarship money to offer to students who would benefit most from our program; and those very students are served best by a small, nurturing, and highly indi-vidualized teacher training experience. Bilingual candidates, who are representative of the majority of students now in Bay Area schools, are the candidates we wanted to add to the pool of teachers who will impact the learners of the next millennia. But how could we do it? How could we make it possible for prospective bilingual teacher candidates to enter our program when many of them had not yet completed a Bachelor's degree?

It was this question we set about to answer, through an innovative partnership arrangement with the Ravenswood City School District and a local community college. This three-partner program, designed to train and certify at least 25 bilingual teachers over a three year period, is currently in its third year of operation, and has proven to be highly effective, surpassing our original expectations.

The purpose of this chapter is to describe what we did, explain how it is working, and provide a model for other institutions. We are convinced that in the future such partnerships are going to be the norm and not the exception. We are further convinced that the quality of our program has been enhanced by including the talented and dedicated group of paraprofessionals from the Ravenswood City School District who, because of this partnership arrangement, can go forward as fully certified teachers.

Innovative Partnership Arrangement: The "Pipeline" Concept

California suffers from an acute shortage of credentialed bilingual teachers. California colleges and universities have been unable to produce sufficient numbers of teachers to meet the need of providing limited English proficient students an equal educational opportunity. This dilemma has significantly impacted the Ravenswood City School District where the LEP student population grew from 25% of the total enrollment in 1987 to 75% in East Palo Alto, in 1994.

Located in the San Francisco Bay Peninsula, the Ravenswood City School District serves a small but diverse community in the cities of East Palo Alto and Menlo Park. Total district enrollment is approximately 4,200 divided among eight different elementary campuses serving kindergarten through eighth grade students.

The East Palo Alto and eastern Menlo Park communities are characterized by poverty, unemployment, and a high rate of drug-related criminal activity. One third of Ravenswood students receive AFDC and 85% of the district pupils qualify for free/reduced price meals. The entire population of the city of East Palo Alto, incorporated in 1983, amounts to just over 23,500, and yet the 2.5 square mile city has the unenviable reputation of having the highest per capita homicide rate in the entire State of California. The dropout rate for Ravenswood students hovers at approximately 65%.

Given the extreme difficulty in attracting experienced qualified bilingual teachers to Ravenswood City School District, the College of Notre Dame, and the primary lower division feeder institution, Cañada College, decided to work together to develop a novel Teacher Training Program with a Cross Cultural Language and Academic Development (CLAD) Emphasis. The Ravenswood City School District and the College of Notre Dame agreed to pursue the funding to make such collaboration possible.

Collaboration: The Inherent Strength

The collaboration began in 1992, when a Ravenswood School District staff member approached the Education Department at College of Notre Dame inquiring if we would be interested in applying for a Title VII Educational Training Program grant award. This grant award, for over one-half million dollars, would be administered by the Office of Bilingual Education and Minority Language Affairs in the U.S. Department of Education. For a period of nine months, representatives of the College of Notre Dame, the Bilingual Education Department of the Ravenswood City School District, and Canada Community College met to design a model career ladder training program that would support paraprofessionals in pursuing college degrees, and provide teacher training for candidates working in Ravenswood bilingual classrooms on emergency credentials.

Because many of these paraprofessionals had not yet finished their undergraduate work, the idea of a "pipeline" was formed, and became the over-riding concept that defined our approach to the problem. The problem, simply stated, was that we needed to increase the pool of bilingual candidates who had completed their undergraduate work before we could increase the numbers who had obtained bilingual teaching credentials in California. To do this, we needed to find a way to provide financial aid for these students. After several meetings, the three-partner collaborative developed the following goals and identified three major areas of concern. The goal statement submitted with the Title VII grant proposal was as follows:

1. To help overcome the tremendous shortage of teachers who are aware of cross cultural and language needs of bilingual children by producing competent professionals to work in classrooms where Limited English Proficient (LEP) children can have an equal opportunity and a chance to reach their full potential.

2. To train and certify at least twenty-five (25) CLAD/BCLAD teachers by providing scholarship help as they "move through the pipeline" of community college coursework, College of Notre Dame's Commission on Teacher Credentialing approved Liberal Studies Program and the Multiple Subject Credential/CLAD certification.

To substantiate the need for the Teacher Training Program with a Cross Cultural emphasis, the College of Notre Dame, Canada College and Ravenswood City School District also identified three major areas of concern:

(1) the extremely large and growing number of limited English proficient students in Peninsula schools;

53

(2) the dramatically increasing demand for teachers who are aware of cross cultural and differing language needs; and

(3) the type of training local education agencies need and the competencies teachers should have to work with LEP students.

These crucial needs were determined from state and federal reports and from local school district data provided to College of Notre Dame by Ravenswood City School District. The following chart provides the detail of scheduled activities and demonstrates the "pipeline" model:

Year 1: July 1, 1993 - June 30, 1994	Timeline in Months (July through June)											
Activity	J	A	S	O	N	D	J	F	M	A	M	J
1. Assign Project personnel	X											
2. Articulate transfer of units between the community College and CND		X										
3. Advise the course of study at both Colleges			X	X								
4. Organize collaborative orientation seminars with trainees			X									
5. Assign coursework for trainees	X	X	X	X	X	X	X	X	X	X	X	X
6. Continue formal relationship with Advisory Committee & Ravenswood City School District		X	X	X	X	X	X	X	X	X	X	X
7. Individual meetings with Trainee Selection committee		X	X	X	X	X	X	X	X	X	X	X
8. Ongoing evaluation and review by outside auditor	X	X	X	X	X	X	X	X	X	X	X	X
9. Exit interview of students										X		
10. Plan next cycle							X	X	X	X	X	X

Enrollment and completion data for the program follow:

Year 1: (1993-1994)
 12 students were enrolled in the Credential Program at CND
 4 students were undergraduate Liberal Studies majors
 7 undergraduate students were at Canada College being advised by the College of Notre Dame Liberal Studies Coordinator
 1 student graduated with a Multiple Subject Credential

Year 2: (1994-1995)
Activities similar to year 1.
 10 students were enrolled in the Credential Program at CND
 5 students were undergraduate Liberal Studies majors

6 undergraduate students were at Canada College being advised by the College of Notre Dame Liberal Studies Coordinator

7 students graduated with a Multiple Subject Credential

Year 3 (1995- 1996)
9 students were enrolled in the Credential Program at CND
4 were undergraduate students
9 students graduated with a Multiple Subject Credential

Since the grant will carry through the fall semester of 1996, we will meet our goal of certification for twenty-five bilingual candidates.

College of Notre Dame's Business Office manages the grant. The College provides centralized administrative services for management of the grant that include purchasing, budget, grant administration, and staff personnel, and all are coordinated with administrative staff in the Education Department. Interim and final fiscal reports to the granting agency are generated as may be required. The Business Office prints out monthly expenditure reports for the Program Coordinator of the Teacher Training Program. The report is printed one month after the expenditure. Therefore, the Program Coordinator keeps a separate journal accounting system which is updated continually for daily accounting purposes.

The Program Coordinator of the Title VII Teacher Training Program meets with the staff on a monthly basis at regular Department meetings to update members on issues pertaining to the Teacher Training Program, to make decisions that affect the Title VII Teacher Training Program, and to coordinate activities. This activity ensures communication among the staff. Through this collaboration, the goals and objectives of the program are jointly established by all staff. Defined areas of responsibility for each staff member are delineated. The results achieved are measured and evaluated against program objectives. In this manner, all staff members review each of the objectives and reach consensus on how each objective is to be attained. This process is successful because:

1. It involves clear, specific identification of desired results.

2. It establishes a realistic strategy in the allocation of program resources to achieve results.

3. Objectives are mutually agreed to by District and College participants.

Budget and Cost Effectiveness

The project requested $517,153 over the three years of the OBEMLA-funded program.

The project was funded at $517,595. It was the only Title VII funded program in California in 1993.

On a year-by-year basis, the cost-benefit is as follows:

Year	OBEMLA Request	Cost/Participant/semester
1-(1993-1994)	$179,782.	$7,191.
2-(1994-1995)	$171,429.	$6,857.
3-(1995-1996)	$166,384.	$6,655.
Totals-3 years	$517,595.	($6,901. Average)

The activities outlined in the Title VII Grant can serve as a model for other IHE/District collaboration. Such activities include but are not limited to:

1. Increasing communication between the Department of Education at College of Notre Dame, Ravenswood City School District and Cañada College;

2. The formation of a collaborative partnership between bilingual education, the Bilingual Multifunctional Resource Centers, and College of Notre Dame;

3. On-going advising provided by the Liberal Studies and the Multiple Subject Credential Coordinators at College of Notre Dame;

4. Providing precision in bilingual teaching methodology, content areas, culture, and establishment of proficiency in Spanish language, and English;

5. Addressing and complementing existing programmatic, curricular and institutional policies with the Department of Education, emphasizing Cross Cultural Education;

6. Updating instructional materials, especially videos on multicultural education;

7. Providing a forum for teaching professionals to assist in understanding bilingual education and the needs of the LEP student;

8. Joint District and College committees review all requests from Ravenswood paraprofessionals who want to be considered for the program.

Conclusion

The College, with Title VII assistance, has been able to provide educational opportunities and assist in the inservice plan of the Ravenswood City School District. The College will continue to provide facilities for teacher training with a cross cultural emphasis so that the Program will continue to be highly visible in the mainstream of the Department of Education's activities. Since the grant was awarded, curriculum modifications, adjustments, and renovations have been made so that we can work more effectively with program participants and our non-program candidates.

The ongoing consultations that College of Notre Dame has had with Ravenswood City School District, Cañada College, other educational programs, and community resources give indications that this collaborative effort in teacher certification can have considerable impact in the State and region. The credentialed bilingual teachers produced by the project not only will assist the public schools in Ravenswood City School District but also certify a cadre of competent teachers who will contribute to the teaching profession as a whole.

In 1995-1996, College of Notre Dame and the Ravenswood City School District will apply for a continuation grant so that more students at an early stage of their college education will have the opportunity to earn a CLAD credential. This will continue to enhance the numbers of bilingual teachers from under-represented groups. A new grant, now being prepared, will be sent to the U.S. Department of Education in Washington D.C. pending release of funds and grant approval. We also will participate in a State of California grant for career-ladder training. Thus we hope to extend the "pipeline approach" for another three years, continuing to meet the needs of children by providing certification for motivated bilingual paraprofessionals and teachers.

As an affirmation of the success of our partnership program, in spring 1995, the Ravenswood City School District and College of Notre Dame Department of Education were awarded the annual Quality of Education Award for Distinguished Service to Children and the Preparation of Teachers.

Partnership for School Renewal: Site-Based Graduate Education Focusing on Individual School Needs

Kay L. Hegler
Richard E. Dudley

Doane College (Nebraska)

In 1992, Doane College implemented a new graduate program leading to a Master of Education degree. During the three-year process of program design, Ralph W. Tyler, Doane Class of 1921, served as a key consultant. In 1989, he presented the education faculty with a charge which has permeated all of the planning and design of the program. Tyler emphasized that meeting the needs of P-12 educators "must" be the central goal of a quality graduate program in education. "Ask the teachers what they want!" Tyler insisted. The charge to listen to the teachers and their administrators has been the central focus of the partnership between the P-12 personnel and Doane Master of Education faculty in the development and implementation of the program.

Tyler's charge was issued at a time when national education leaders and antagonists alike were focusing on the need for systemic educational renewal and transformation. The need to provide positive growth experiences for P-12 teachers and to strengthen linkages between P-12 education and college/university faculty was recognized by John Goodlad in *Teachers for Our Nation's Schools* and was reflected in the standards set by the National Council for Accreditation of Teacher Education (NCATE).

In keeping with Tyler's suggestion to "Ask the teachers what they want," the Education Department sent out a questionnaire related to teachers' needs for graduate education. Respondents emphasized all of the following: (1) a degree emphasizing classroom application of current research in their classrooms; (2) courses located closer to their homes and schools; (3) a faculty alert to the daily challenges facing P-12 teachers; (4) a faculty committed to helping identify alternative educational solutions appropriate for each school setting; (5) the opportunity to leave every graduate class session with at least one new idea to implement in their classrooms as well as the rationale for the change; and, (6) a graduate course schedule reflective of the K-12 academic calendar.

The full-time faculty members in teacher education were committed to developing a program responsive to each of the needs expressed by the teachers responding to the survey. They were also guided by the postulates set forth by John Goodlad; and, consistent with Doane's undergraduate program, they voluntarily chose to design a program that would meet or exceed all of the NCATE standards. The purpose of this chapter is to describe the program, the process used for the development of the graduate sites, and the elements of partnership embodied in the program design.

Collaborative Program Components

In responding to the needs expressed by P-12 personnel and placing importance on the concept of collaboration, the faculty planning team determined that: (1) the program would be site-based at school settings demonstrating an interest in graduate study and change; (2) a core set of courses totalling 15 credits would provide grounding for the conceptual framework; (3) over half of the 36 credits of the program would be from elective courses designed specifically to meet the needs of the teachers at the site; (4) full-time faculty in the Doane teacher education program and selected adjunct faculty would form a single faculty roster to present the program at all sites; (5) site-based advising would be done by the full-time faculty; (6) the culminating experience of a project or thesis could be done collaboratively by two or more students in the program; (7) yearly dissemination of research completed by the graduate students would be handled through a special publication, *The Orange Book*; (8) arts and science faculty would be asked to collaboratively develop courses for this program in curriculum and instruction in areas related to the identified subject area needs of elementary and secondary teachers; and, (9) there would be careful attention to developing ways for Doane faculty to work in partnership with teachers and administrators at the graduate sites.

Site-Based Settings

Each of the ten school districts currently serving as sites has requested of Doane to be recognized as a site. Prior to the formal recognition as a site, the Dean of Graduate Studies in Education has met with the K-12 teachers, the principal(s), superintendent, and in most cases members of the school board. The series of meetings with those personnel is used to define the unique needs of the potential site, review the school's mission statement, and look at the district's strategic plan. A comprehensive plan of action for graduate study with elective courses emphasizing the identified needs of the school with clear attention to undergirding the district's mission and the strategic plan has been a key to the success of the individual sites.

A stated interest in change rather than strategic location has been the guiding principle for establishing the sites. Most sites are within a three-hour driving distance of the Doane campus to lend some ease to the management system in place for each site. The Graduate Dean in Education visits all sites at least three times each semester. These visits help to coordinate the program at the site, assist in determining the schedule of courses for the upcoming terms, and allow for the important communication component in maintaining collaboration between Doane and the site.

Nebraska is essentially a rural state. Two sites are located in the most urban areas of Nebraska, Lincoln and metropolitan Omaha. The other sites are in communities ranging in population from 2500 to 35,000. Most of the current sites are within one and one-half hours of travel from Doane. However, two require in excess of two hours of travel one way.

Core Courses

The core courses are Improvement of Instruction, Critical Issues, Assessment of Learning Outcomes or Advanced Whole Language, Research Methods, and Culminating Project or Thesis. These courses provide the grounding for the program's conceptual framework, "The Developing Professional." They support the four main outcomes of the program: (1) to use teaching processes, (2) to foster critical thinking, (3) to consider individual learners, and (4) to develop personal and professional competencies. The indicators delineated for each of these outcomes reflect the department's constructivist philosophy.

Elective Courses

Of the 36 credit hours required to complete the program, 21 are electives. These electives are collaboratively designed by the teachers and administrators at the site and Doane full-time faculty. They provide the undergirding for the changes the district personnel have identified as important for their own school improvement. For example, one school moved toward an emphasis in computers and technology; another toward curriculum design and assessment; a third centered their electives on inclusive education practices; and another selected the transition to middle grades from junior high as a link between the primary and secondary programs. Each of these emphases identified by the school personnel at the site provided the platform for a series of elective courses for the individual site.

The needs of any one school do influence the total graduate program. Once courses are developed for a specific site, at the request of another site, the courses may be offered in other locations. Additionally, when a school district is accepted as a site, it agrees that graduate students from outside the district may attend the graduate courses offered at the site. However, the elective curriculum is primarily determined by the teachers/administrators at the site. The central focus of those electives is to assist the school district serving as a site in making the changes it has identified as significant.

Consistent with the college-wide policy on new courses, the M.Ed. program is able to offer these "unique to the district" courses twice as Selected Topics courses. To offer the course more than twice, the course must be approved by the Graduate academic Affairs Committee and the full-time faculty of the College. Because many of the electives developed for one site are based on nationally recognized areas of school renewal, Selected Topics offerings frequently are viewed as beneficial to more than one site and are developed into courses offered at most but not necessarily all sites.

Most commonly these elective courses are taught by adjunct faculty with exceptional expertise in the area and a background of experiences related to the Special Topic. Once developed, the course may be taught by either the same faculty member at each site or any one of several faculty qualified to teach that specific course.

The Faculty

There are nine full-time faculty in the Unit. These faculty are primarily responsible for teaching in the undergraduate program. Six of them serve as advisors to the graduate students. Those six have been identified by the College as Graduate Faculty and each has a three-credit hour reduced load one semester each year.

The adjunct faculty are all practitioners from area school districts. All were identified as outstanding educators in their own school district with exceptional expertise in the course(s) they were asked to teach. The criteria for selection as an adjunct faculty member include the recognition as an outstanding educator within the individual's own school district, a graduate degree, a doctoral degree or exceptional expertise in the area of graduate instruction, and acceptance of the Doane Teacher Education conceptual framework. Currently four of the adjunct faculty were recruited as a result of their outstanding performance as graduate students in the program.

While some adjunct teach only one course a year, during the 1995 spring, summer, and fall terms nine taught at least one course in each of the three terms and eight taught in two of the three terms. Each has received permission from his/her school district to serve as an adjunct and in almost every school district the adjunct is encouraged by the administration to pursue this professional development activity.

Full-time faculty and adjunct faculty collaborate in several different settings. They teach side-by-side at each site and work collaboratively in those settings. They meet formally once each year to discuss the program, review the conceptual framework, and work on issues of concern. Both adjunct and full-time faculty have access to the same travel funds for professional growth. This has led to attendance at several professional meetings both within Nebraska and outside the State jointly attended by the adjunct and full-time faculty. For example, in 1995 two full-time faculty and three adjunct faculty members attended the International Whole Language Conference in Windsor, Ontario, and jointly presented; two adjunct and one full-time faculty member attended the annual 4-MAT conference in Minneapolis; two adjunct attended the cooperative learning conference in California; and two other adjuncts attended an international conference on gifted education. Each of these experiences was partially or fully funded by the graduate budget.

Site-Based Advising

Each graduate student is assigned an advisor among the full-time faculty. The faculty believe that site-based advising is one way to provide personal contact with each graduate student, a value consistent with a small, private liberal arts college.

Site-based advising primarily takes place in one of the following two ways. First, if the faculty member advising that site is assigned to teach a course at the site, advising happens before or after nearly every class session. This allows time for information to be exchanged and processed. The other format occurs if the faculty member plans an after-school advising session at the school site. In those settings the advisees are notified of these meetings by letter. Because each site is likely to have teachers enrolled from multiple schools, it is almost always necessary for the advisor to visit several schools to do "site-based" advising. In addition many graduate advisees and advisors use e-mail as an effective and efficient strategy for advising. Phone calls are common and undergird the advising system. However, the personal contact is so important to the process it is always present.

The Culminating Project/Thesis

Each student must complete a culminating project or thesis addressing a specific need within his/her own classroom or school. Students from a building or district often elect to work collaboratively on a culminating project. For example, nine students who were kindergarten teachers from Grand Island redesigned the kindergarten curriculum for that District to make it more developmentally appropriate. Five students from Fremont designed and implemented a plan for inclusion; four students from Norfolk redesigned the assessment plan for the elementary schools in the District to incorporate more attention on portfolios; and, five students from Elmwood-Murdock developed and implemented a program to emphasize writing across the curriculum in the secondary school. These collaborative efforts on the projects have been consistent with the changes identified by teachers and administrators in the planning meetings set up to design the programs for each site. They have served to enhance the efforts for change.

The Orange Book

Collaboration is also reflected by Doane's efforts to disseminate the research findings of its graduate students. *The Orange Book* is published annually, containing a 250-word abstract of each culminating project or thesis completed during the previous academic year. The abstracts are written by the graduate student at the conclusion of the project or thesis. One copy of *The Orange Book* is mailed to each school district in Nebraska. It serves as the primary vehicle for distribution of the findings of the M.Ed. program's graduates.

Collaboration with Arts and Sciences

Although the Doane Master of Education degree is in curriculum and instruction, it has been responsive to the requests for courses in content areas. The majority of these requests have come from secondary teachers; however, elementary teachers are also seeking to enhance knowledge and process related to subject area instruction. Courses in music, math, natural science, computers, and history were offered in the summer of 1995. Each of these courses was taught by a full-time member of the Doane faculty in that content area.

K-12 opportunities for Doane Faculty

The Doane teacher education faculty have capitalized on several opportunities to collaborate with P-12 personnel on projects. One has recently published a software program for management of primary grade-level portfolios jointly developed with a graduate student at one of the sites. Another is involved in a three-year on-going assessment of teacher's attitudes toward inclusion and changes in practice for inclusive education. One is engaged in a longitudinal study of the graduate program's outcomes working with a research team of three graduates of the program. Four have provided in-service presentations to P-12 faculty resulting from the contacts made during graduate courses. Two have participated in collaborative teaching projects emerging from the graduate course contacts. Four have team-taught one or more graduate courses with P-12 personnel.

Evaluation

On-going formative evaluation of this program has been a focus of the faculty. The evaluation process has included the initial NCATE accreditation visit, case analyses of change at individual school sites, annual data from graduates in the M.Ed. Graduate Questionnaire, a short questionnaire sent to principals of recent graduates, review of the number of graduate students in the program each year, and review of the number of school districts interested in selection as a site.

During the April 1995 NCATE Board of Examiner's initial review of this program, the visitation team recognized the program as exemplary. The BOE report states:

> In the judgment of the BOE, the quality of this graduate program, its effectiveness in creating dynamic change in the classroom, of generating genuine excitement for teaching among teachers, its sagacious mix of higher education faculty and exceptionally qualified practicing teachers in adjunct roles, and its delivering of the programs in such a manner as to enable teachers to apply learning immediately in their own classrooms, represents a model of professional graduate degree programming which should be emulated for teachers everywhere.

Conclusion

Collaboration with K-12 schools is a reality in the M.Ed. program in curriculum and instruction. This partnership is best described by program graduates in comments added to the Program Graduates' Questionnaire. One graduate wrote, "This program was precisely what I needed to enhance and enrich my twenty-one years of teaching! It brought me up-to-date and into the future. Fellow teachers accepted the new ideas and worked happily with me even though it was difficult finding the time and energy at times. The (K-12) students were very enthusiastic and happy with integrating art and social studies and asked if they'd get to do it next year too! The core and elective classes I took complemented one another and created great research and background for my successful culminating project. Yes, I am working on another project with another teacher and class—my goal is one a year!" A second graduate noted, "The program was an exceptional one and really catered to the needs of the (graduate) students. The convenience of on-site classes was a great advantage." And, a third wrote, "For the first time in any part of my college career the classes were meaningful, practical, and really in touch with the real issues of what teaching is all about. Doane taught me a lot in a safe non-threatening environment. An environment where working together to achieve your best was the goal." This partnership is making a positive difference in the lives of K-12 students in Nebraska and in the lives of their teachers.

Pen Pals

Joanna R. Jones
Kimberly Clem

Grand Canyon University (Arizona)

L anguage skills used consistently and effectively need to be taught and practiced in context (Pappas, Keifer, & Levstik, 1993; Weaver, 1995). During the 1994-1995 school year, a pen pal letter exchange project was established between language arts preservice teachers from Grand Canyon University, Phoenix, and seventh grade students at Harold Smith Magnet School, Glendale, a low socioeconomic population. The purpose of this partnership was for students to participate in an authentic writing experience. The seventh grade class, primarily Hispanic, contained fifteen bilingual students who were at various stages of acquiring English skills. Another five students in a gifted program and three students receiving special educational services participated.

As an elementary school component, parents must be notified and aware of the program. The parent response was extremely positive. One parent bought a three-ring binder to hold all of the letters his son received and copies of the one he wrote. The parent also requested that pen pals meet face to face sometime throughout the year. The parent was impressed with the program. He appreciated the enthusiasm his son expressed with receiving letters and discussing the topics.

Management of the Partnership

Initial letters of introduction as recommended by Block (1993) and written by the preservice teachers to the seventh grade students began the exchange at the beginning of the school year. This was the only letter writing assignment to be completed during any class time. All remaining letters were written as homework assignments. Exchanges took place on a weekly basis; letters were delivered and returned to the seventh grader teacher's mailbox. The frequency of the letter exchanges was critical to keep a fluent conversation going between pen pals as well as to maintain a high interest level for all participants. As a result, both groups of students eagerly anticipated receiving letters.

The second letter exchange included a Polaroid picture. This experience was one of the highlights of the pen pal project. Being able to put a face to the person to whom students were writing added a visual dimension to the writing process. Classroom dialogue included comparisons on the physical attributes of their pen pals. At one point, the seventh grade students were so fixated on what the preservice teachers looked like that the seventh grade students disregarded what had been written and made judgments based on appearances. Over the course of the pen pal experience, students worked through the issues of the importance of appearance versus the quality of the letter writing ability.

A critical decision made by both instructors was that none of the letters would be read or graded by the instructors. The preservice teachers received a participation grade while the seventh grade students received homework credit for having written a letter. Not reviewing the letters benefited both groups as they became focused on the communication process. Letters could be a draft or a final revised product, a decision that was up to the students. During the course of the year, concerns surfaced that related to student accountability and moral issues; however, in this project, the decision was made to put the trust in the students (Calkins, 1994; Calkins & Harwayne, 1987; Weaver, 1994). To further demonstrate the trust, all letters were placed in individual envelopes. Students readily shared in class discussions items of concern or out-of-the-ordinary type comments. Therefore, data were collected only through conversations and observations.

Although class sizes were uneven, several of the seventh grade students volunteered to write to more than one preservice teacher. Interest in letter writing was expressed by some of the seventh grade students who would never consider extra writing assignments. In truth, "at-risk" students with multiple pen pals were acquiring English language skills. A couple of the seventh grade students participated in letter writing when they would not do any other writing. From their group comments, they perceived letter writing as a social event free from critique.

During the first semester, a couple of students from both sides, did not willingly follow through with letter writing. These authentic experiences made it difficult to insist that students write letters when they had not received letters. Absences and illnesses contributed to some breakdown between pen pals. To avoid letter exchange problems the second semester, students were asked to sign-off on a list when letters were submitted.

Planning and Integrating Curriculum

As with any collaborative project, a great deal of communication is required on the part of the instructors. Initial planning was on the management of the physical exchange of letters. On the third exchange of letters, the instructors began discussing the students' comments which had been heard. Connections about student abilities were noticed: spelling patterns reflective of learners of English as a second language, writing with topic sentences, grammar, and letter form. Plans to connect the integration of other curricular areas were considered and backgrounds on classroom projects were built.

Poetry was woven into lessons for both classes. The preservice teachers were learning about a variety of formula poetry such as haiku, cinquain, color poems, and repeated beginnings. In the letters to the seventh grade students, the preservice teachers described one or more types of poetry. Some of the descriptions were followed with samples written by the preservice teachers. Hurrying to finish their letters and not considering the power of their modelling, several preservice teachers stuck the information onto the end of their letters. The seventh grade students noticed this inconsistency in the flow of the letters. They made comments like, "Where did this come from?" "This doesn't make any sense?" "This poem's dumb!" and "What's this?" During a poetry unit which focused on free form poetry, the seventh grade students aggressively discussed what they thought poetry should be. They determined that poetry was conveying vivid thoughts and feelings with words. They found it difficult to accept formula poetry. Cognitive dissonance fueled both classroom discussions and personal creativity. Seven of the seventh grade students' pieces of poetry won at their grade level in the state poetry contest. Having received a color poem, one seventh grade girl wanting to please her preservice teacher, invested in color pens and wrote her next letter in a rainbow appearance.

A final topic through the integrated curriculum was reading World War II literature. The preservice teachers and seventh grade students read *Sadako and the Thousand Paper Crane* (Coerr, 1977), *The Faithful Elephants* (Tsuchiya, 1988), *Hiroshima, No Pika* (Maruki, 1980), *Number the Stars* (Lowry, 1989), and *Devil's Arithmetic* (Yolen, 1990). Within the language arts program, the preservice teachers were learning multiple ways books can enhance the understanding of grammar skills and literary elements. Within the seventh grade program, the students were learning how the events of World War II could happen. Seventh grade students were allotted bonus points for reading World War II novels. Their reading program was individualized and included a reading contract for a nine-week period. Notably, when the pen pals wrote about the books, they didn't retell a story; instead, themes and issues about the concept of war emerged, "grand conversations" (Peterson & Eeds, 1989). Those new concepts were incorporated into class discussions on the topic. Two of the pen pals became engrossed in pages and pages of discussion about Jewish holocaust survivors. The preservice teacher had worked in a home where she interacted with survivors. She shared experiences and stories with the seventh grade student who in turn asked more questions and shared the stories with classmates. The topic became so real to the seventh grader! It became obvious that no other classroom experience could achieve that depth of inquiry.

Partnership Challenges

The pen pal letter exchange project presented a number of challenges to the partnership. Having to perform as teachers, the preservice teachers often did not know what topics to discuss with the seventh grade students. During class discussion, returning university students who have teenage children suggested ideas like clothing, music and movies. Younger preservice teachers chimed in with topic ideas from younger brothers and sisters or cousins. Movies, books, radio stations, and personal activities began to emerge. The preservice teachers talked about authentic topics and age appropriate concerns.

When the preservice teachers filled their letters with a list of questions, the seventh grade students often provided their responses to these questions with one word sentences, "blue." No sentence structure was used in the response; sentence numbering was omitted; the friendly letter format became a vertical column of answers.

Some letters were very short. Several times seventh grade students wrote, "I'm too busy right now. I'll write more later." The preservice teachers were disappointed; they felt that short letters were a way for the seventh grade students to say that they were disinterested in the project but still wanting to get credit for participation.

One seventh grade student inadvertently placed the preservice teacher's letter into the envelope where the new letter should have been. The preservice teacher, when he received the letter, was surprised and wrote back to the student about the occurrence. This same pair complained several times that the other member didn't write very much or hadn't sent a letter. However, in the face to face meeting later in the semester, these two students made the best personal communication connection and talked at length during the times the groups were together.

One of the preservice teachers dropped the language arts class in the fall semester but registered for the class again in the spring semester. Knowing the importance of having a continued friendship, she did not drop the communication with the pen pal. Each week the preservice teacher made a stop by the professor's office to pick up the letter and to write a reply. She had nine months of communication with the student.

One of the seventh grade boys had a preservice pen pal who dropped the course the first semester. Then while taking the course again in the second semester, the preservice teacher decided to leave the teaching career. She did not leave because of the seventh grader, but her action did impact him since no further letters were exchanged. When the instructor stressed the importance of helping someone make a better career choice, the boy appeared to take the events all in stride.

An age-old topic which generated interest was weddings. During each semester one preservice teacher got married. The brides-to-be wrote long letters filled with a great deal of information about their upcoming events. The pen pals wrote two or more pages in reply. The brides-to-be sent pictures both before and after the weddings.

Controversial topics brought concern to the preservice teachers. The seventh grade students were describing their friends of the opposite sex. One of the seventh grade girls had a new boyfriend every two weeks. The preservice teacher wanted to know how much to comment about the topic. Another preservice teacher received a letter describing a hate for police.

One topic for a letter especially surprised the instructors. A preservice teacher asked the seventh grade pen pal for advice about her situation: she was getting a divorce, parenting one child, and needing to work. The instructor's response was to guide the seventh grade student's thoughts about the letter and to write a personal opinion in response. The student wrote about when his dad left his mom.

Culminating Activities

Letter exchanges continued for another twelve weeks at which time pen pals met face to face. In the face to face meeting in December, the preservice teachers went to visit the seventh grade students. It was a spontaneous visit at the preservice students' convenience through out an eight-day period. The preservice teachers came in small groups or pairs or alone. They would come to the seventh grade classroom and introduce themselves and meet their pen pals. Seventh grade students suddenly became extremely shy and red faced. The "talkers" and "doers" suddenly didn't know what to do. The preservice students were surprised at the socioeconomic setting of the students. The initial portion of the meeting was extremely tense as preservice teachers just took the seventh grade students to the picnic table area to talk. A few had lunch with their pen pal. After about one-third of the way into the time spent together, the pairs became more comfortable with the conversation and common dialogue from the letters became the center of the discussion.

In a second face-to-face meeting in April, the seventh grade students came to the university. Their visit included lunch, a tour of the university, a demonstration of the physioanatomy lab, participation in a club meeting, and participation in organized literary activities. Face-to-face conversations connected common experiences. The benefits for students were enormous. The university setting helped seventh grade students see real people in college. They knew ordinary people in college. College was within their reach. In fact, many of the seventh grade students made comments about "When I go to college . . ."

Assessment/Evaluation

The instructors learned about students in both classes through "kid-watching" (Marek, et al, 1984) and facilitating student discussion (Peterson & Eeds, 1989). Students' ability to critique peer writing increased. Relevant issues were articulated more clearly as students discussed among themselves topics of grammar and content.

Preservice teachers were expected to write an evaluation of their individual student's communication skills. These evaluations were responded to by the instructors for both accuracy of evaluation and use of professional language. The importance of identifying and building on strengths of students was stressed. Weaknesses were easily located but communicating these through positive language stretched the preservice teachers. The seventh grade students were not exposed to the evaluation from their pen pals.

In Arizona, this partnership was authentically preparing the seventh grade students for the Arizona Student Assessment Plan (ASAP) language elements which requires performance accuracy in written communication (Arizona Department of Education, 1987). In the current project, students will evaluate the preservice teachers' letters and form rubrics much like the ASAP. These rubrics will also be self-evaluation rubrics. Then the responsibility and accountability for the letter writing will be back on the shoulders of the students. Plans are also underway to add electronic mail as a dimension of computer literacy for this project.

This year-long project demonstrated that some of the weakest writers in the seventh grade class took on two and three pen pals. Successful pen pal partners were not necessarily the best writers or the people with the most in common. The successful partners were the partners that wrote about real issues and real concerns. They were authentic and the concern, care or interest in the topic they were writing about came through in their letters and made their partners want to respond. They wanted an authentic reason for writing.

Conclusion

Both groups gained from this pen pal project. The preservice teachers were impacted by the great diversity of learning among students within one classroom. Preservice teachers frequently talked about the power in the thinking abilities of their partners and the worldliness of the lives of the students. Preservice teachers in elementary education do not regularly select junior high grades in which to complete practica; however, through this project, a new level of appreciation for this age group was found.

The seventh grade students became aware of possible careers. Throughout the school year, their language increasingly included the phrase, "When I go to college." Visiting the university allowed the students to break college-bound only barriers and helped them to envision the reality of those careers. Students who would not otherwise write became avid writers. Writing skills of the seventh grade students improved. Through the enthusiasm of the seventh grade class, Harold Smith Magnet School had an all-school letter exchange program during the last weeks of the school year.

Similarities emerged which indicated that letter writing holds a great deal of value in the language arts curriculum. First, both groups could hardly wait to get their letters. This task of communication required a "need" to receive a reply. Secondly, only topics of importance warranted a courteous response. Other topics were ignored, answered in brevity or stated as a "dumb idea" to the writer. Third, both groups found power in the written word instead of the visual or oral worlds. Finally, the letters did establish friendships.

References

Arizona Department of Education. (1989). *Arizona language arts essential skills*. Phoenix: Author.

Block, C. C. (1993). *Teaching the language arts: Expanding thinking through student-centered instruction*. Boston: Allyn and Bacon.

Calkins, L. M. (1994). *The art of teaching writing*. Portsmouth, NJ: Heinemann.

Calkins, L. M. & Harwayne, S. (1987). *The writing workshop: A world of difference*. Portsmouth, NH: Heineman.

Coerr, E. C. (1977). *Sadako and the thousand paper cranes*. New York: Dell.

Lowry, L. (1989). *Number the stars*. Boston: Houghton Mifflin.

Marek, A., Howard, D., Disinger, J., Jacobson, D., Earle, N., Goodman, Y., Hood. W., Woodley, C., Woodley, J., Wortman, J., & Wortman. R. (1984). "A kid-watching guide: Evaluation for whole language classrooms." (Occasional Paper No. 9) Tucson, AZ: University of Arizona, Arizona Center for Research and Development.

Maruki, T. (1980). *Hiroshima, no pika*. New York: Lothrop.

Pappas, C. C., Kiefer, B. Z., & Levstik, L. S. (1990). *An integrated language perspective in the elementary school: Theory into action*. New York: Longman.

Peterson, R., & Eeds, M. (1989). *Grand conversations*. New York: Scholastic.

Tsuchiya, U. (1988). *Faithful elephants*. Boston: Houghton Mifflin.

Weaver, C. (1995). *Facts on teaching skills in context*. Michigan English language arts framework project. Lancing, MI: Michigan Department of Education.

Weaver, C. (1994). *Reading process and practice: From socio-psycholinguistics to whole language*. Porsmouth, NH: Heinemann.

Yolen, J. (1990). *The devil's arithmetic*. New York: Puffin.

College-School Partnership to Improve Teacher Preparation at Grinnell College

Martha Voyles, Beryl Wellborn, Cheryl Rotert, Sue Sears, Chris Day, Deborah Charnetski, Marsha Bachman, and Doug Cameron

Grinnell College (Iowa)

A saying that pokes fun at teachers and especially at college methods faculty is, "Those who can, do. Those who can't, teach. Those who can't teach, teach teachers." Like many jokes, it relies on a perception of truth for its humor. Public school teachers and preservice teachers do sometimes consider faculty in a college Education Department to be far removed from the reality of day to day teaching in today's K-12 classrooms. Likewise, it is a rare meeting of college methods instructors that doesn't bemoan the swiftness with which student teachers forget all the principles they learned in their methods courses. Both groups know that such attitudes reflect a limited perspective, but the grumbling continues and periodically captures the attention of legislators and educational reformers. Thus, the solutions proliferate. States require prospective teachers to spend more field experience hours in "real" classrooms, presumably to make up for deficits in their college courses, or require college faculty to spend some minimal amount of time teaching in K-12 classrooms, presumably for the same reasons. Practicing teachers are required to take additional post graduate course work, and college Education Departments form partnerships with "clinical schools." These and other remedies no doubt help, but a genuine solution continues to elude us.

The reason is not that we haven't yet found the right solution. Nor is it that the problem is intractable. It is a subtle and complex matter, one that is part misunderstanding, part different perspective, and part

74

genuine disagreement. In fact, if we could clear up our misunderstandings and see better the other's perspective, then we would have developed a relationship in which any genuine differences could be out in the open. Open and thoughtful interaction between classroom teachers and methods faculty should lead to professional growth for teachers and college faculty alike. More importantly, such interactions could serve as models of dynamic, productive professional relationships for our preservice teachers. Such relationships do exist, and this chapter illustrates an example, but the norm is a much more limited sort of cooperation that has situation specific goals rather than an overriding mutually developed and conceptualized "point of view."

The difference in perspectives between methods instructors and school teachers creates a serious lack of continuity in most teacher preparatory programs. Typically, there is course work on the one hand and student teaching on the other. Despite major efforts on the part of most college faculty to make the course work and related field experiences an obvious preparation for student teaching, we often hear students teach and their cooperating teachers express the opinion that it is really during student teaching that one learns what one needs to know about teaching.

Several years ago a group of elementary school teachers and two Grinnell colleagues received a grant from the Iowa Department of Education to develop a college-school partnership that would design and implement field experiences for preservice teachers in Grinnell College's teacher preparation program. Our goal was to provide a field experience that would bridge the gap between college classroom learning and student teaching. It was an opportunity for students to implement their methods course work in a real classroom with more guidance and support than they have in the typical student teaching experience and more teaching responsibility than they have in earlier field experiences.

It is common for education departments to plan field experiences for their students. It is less common for the college faculty and teachers in the field experience classrooms to have much substantive interaction. Any communication that does take place is typically about the parameters of the experience such as number of required hours, schedule, expectations of preservice students and possibly evaluation by the classroom teacher.

Immediately after school was out in June, five teachers, one principal, and two Grinnell College methods instructors met together for six hours a day for a week. The grant paid a stipend to all of the participants for this planning time. The first thing that we did was to discuss our position on the available sources of information about "best practice." We discussed the role of information from educational research versus the information teachers obtain through reflection on their own practice and came to a position that was acceptable to all of us. No one believed that "best practice" would rely solely on one or the other source, but we did differ in the relative weight we gave to the sources, with the expected differences between college faculty members and teachers and with a range of opinion among the teachers themselves. We did not necessarily finish this discussion in complete agreement, but it was important to talk about differences openly and to agree that it would be a narrow minded teacher who relied on only one source of information to the exclusion of the other. It was important for the teachers to know that the college faculty believe that their knowledge from years of experience is a critical source of information and for all of us to discuss the role of research and when and how it can inform practice. To some extent all of our subsequent discussions could be said to have been a refinement of our position on this issue in the context of specific areas of instruction. Once we had developed some consensus on the general issue, the college faculty took responsibility for briefly summarizing the research literature in the areas of classroom interaction, classroom management, and the teaching of mathematics, reading, science, and social studies. From there the group wrote a brief list of criteria for best practice in each area. The list was clearly grounded in the research, but it included criteria suggested by teachers, and much of our discussion focused on developing consensus around the precise wording of each of the criteria. When we were finished, the teachers suggested that we needed a section on instructional planning, so we added that.

While finding time for such discussion is difficult, it was perhaps the single most important aspect of the partnership. We found ourselves to be in substantial agreement in all areas with many seeming disagreements turning out to be matters of perspective or language. It was because of these discussions and the document that we produced together that we were able to speak with confidence to the students during their field experiences, and, even more importantly, that we were able to disagree in ways that maintained our professional relationships and did not devalue the opinions or expertise of either college faculty or practicing teachers.

In addition to developing a brief booklet of best practice criteria, we spent time each day developing the best structure for the field experiences. While such joint planning between school and college faculty is not unique, it is too often not done, or done with only one teacher representative, so that other teachers participating in a partnership have very little ownership in the model that is developed. The teachers were unanimous in their belief that preservice students needed more experience actually teaching rather than observing, and the college faculty concurred. Our goal was to design a field experience that constituted a good intermediate experience between college course work and accompanying field experiences that consisted of observation, small group work, or an occasional large group presentation and full-fledged student teaching. We saw the leap from college classes to student teaching as too great and a serious gap in our program. Thus, we wanted to design a field experience that would be guided practice for student teaching.

Features of the Field Experience Model

The model that we developed has five distinguishing features: (1) preservice students work in pairs to plan, write, and teach their lessons; (2) the classroom teachers and college methods instructor review the lesson plans together, and students make revisions; (3) other methods students who are working on the unit but not teaching on a particular day attend and watch; (4) after the lesson preservice students who taught, students who observed, the classroom teacher and the faculty methods instructor have a discussion together about the lesson; (5) the students who taught the lesson have an opportunity to revise the lesson and teach it again. What follows is a description of the model that we developed and how it works.

As part of each of their methods courses (reading, math, social studies, and science) preservice students work in small groups to plan a short unit of instruction. The teacher selects the unit, specifies the number of days the unit should take, and outlines important objectives. Often the teacher provides students with curricular materials or activities that have been used, and students usually observe the class once or twice prior to teaching the unit. The group and methods instructor meet together once to make an overall plan for each day of the unit and to divide up the writing of the actual plans. Students then work in pairs to write detailed plans for two to four of the lessons in the unit. The main advantage of students working in pairs is that partners hold each other accountable for principles they have learned in their methods course. Partners challenge each other with questions such as, "Is this really an experiment or is it just a cook book activity to demonstrate what students already know?" and "Do we have some higher level questions in this discussion?" Such review in a practical setting is critical; it is something that students need to practice before they can do it reliably on their own. If they don't learn it before student teaching begins, it is the kind of thinking they are apt to skip during student teaching in the immediacy of needing something, anything, to do for the next day's lessons. In this field experience students have the luxury of concentrating on one really good unit of instruction. While some might argue that this situation is not true to life, it seemed to us that we were simply following our own guidelines about good practice, breaking the task of teaching into manageable parts for our students and helping them master that process first before tackling something more difficult.

Written lesson plans are submitted to the methods instructor and the classroom teacher about one week before the unit is to start. The teacher and methods instructor both make comments on the students' plans, and that process usually involves their getting together or at least talking by phone and making some joint decisions about various aspects of the plans. For us, these conversations are always intellectually stimulating because we are working with peers on something we both know and care a lot about—good teaching. We learn a lot from these conversations and often use what we learn in teaching. We rely on the classroom teacher's judgment about timing, level of instruction, and a host of other considerations. Lesson plans are returned to the students with comments, and they make revisions accordingly and resubmit their plans for final approval. Such careful feedback and work on plans is not as likely to be a regular part of student teaching; our goal is that by then the new teachers will have internalized the criteria to the extent that they can critique and revise their own plans.

When the day comes to begin teaching the unit, the novice teachers alternate between the excitement of finally getting to do what they have spent several years preparing for and the unavoidable nervousness. The students who wrote the plan for the day teach it together, dividing teaching in any way they want. Having a peer beside them for support and to help out when they can't find something or have trouble getting the overhead focused is just what some students need the first time or two in front of a class. The classroom teacher, methods instructor, and other preservice students who are working on this particular unit observe. Students who are observing sometimes perform assigned tasks such as counting the number and kinds of questions asked or tallying who is called on and how many times by gender or location in the classroom or charting the teachers' movement around the room. At first, we worried that all these extra people in the classroom would affect the behavior of the young students, but they have proved to be much more flexible than the adults. Preservice students watching and learning from peers is one of the real strengths of the model. An experienced teacher makes it all look so easy that students can get a mistaken impression of what is involved. Watching another novice gives a realistic idea of the problems involved and enhances self-confidence because students see that others have concerns and problems similar to their own.

When the lesson is over, we all sit down to discuss it tactfully, kindly, and frankly. After all, this is initial practice, and no one can be expected to do everything perfectly the first time. The students who taught begin the discussion, and the student observers offer their insights. If the teacher and supervisor agree about a particular observation, that is persuasive. More often, we identify the same concern, but have different suggestions. That gives students two different perspectives. Sometimes we disagree. Once that would have been awkward for both, especially in front of the students, but we have developed a working relationship that enables us to do this without finding it threatening. We explain our reasoning and expect students to do the same when they talk about their own practice. If we want students to learn to reflect on their own practice and analyze their teaching by considering principles from course work and their observations, then it is important for us to model that process and give them an opportunity to practice it. The post-mortem on the lesson fosters a joint problem solving approach that is often less threatening than an individual conference during student teaching. It will teach students skills that they will continue to use throughout their careers.

After our discussion students have an opportunity to revise the lesson and teach it again to another group of students. This is possible because in our school district two teachers at a particular grade level often divide the responsibility for teaching various subjects, and each teacher teaches particular subjects to both classes. In student teaching it is more often the case that students receive feedback and are expected to apply it to future lessons, rather than the same lesson. That adds a level of complexity that makes it more difficult for students to benefit from the feedback.

The second time through the lesson is without fail better than the first, so all students are able to demonstrate their learning and to experience success. We used to receive the comment from student teachers that our program needed to provide more experience in classrooms, but now they report that they were well prepared for student teaching. They have already faced some of the common problems that are the undoing of student teachers: getting the attention of a chattering group of students, dealing with a class working in groups with manipulatives, or responding effectively to wrong answers. Of course, they have much left to learn, as do those of us with years of experience; but they have begun to build a repertoire of good teaching practices that they can call on readily during student teaching.

As part of their unit the preservice students are required to plan some kind of evaluation of the classroom students' learning. Whether it is a test or project, the preservice teachers are often more nervous about the outcome than the young students. In the end, they feel, this is the true test of their teaching effectiveness. They are often surprised that not everyone has learned everything, but such a conclusion in itself is a learning experience that spurs them to think about ways to make their lessons and units even better. If the classroom teacher asks them for copies of some of their materials when they have finished teaching, they feel that they have been paid the supreme compliment and have truly joined the ranks of professional teachers.

Houghton College and the King Center School

Charles E. Massey
Claity Price Massey

Houghton College (New York)

Introduction

Houghton College, a four-year co-educational church-related liberal arts institution, serves 1260 students at its main campus in Houghton, New York and 140 students at its extension campus in West Seneca, New York, a suburb of Buffalo. Approximately 225 students are enrolled in the teacher education program. An isolated rural college with a very homogeneous population, Houghton faces special challenges in preparing teachers for work in schools where diversity is increasing and multi-cultural and multi-ethnic understanding is essential. For the past eight years the college has been seeking solutions to its geographic and cultural isolation. The following chronicles the development of a variety of partnerships that have evolved as a result of our search.

Background

In the spring of 1987 Houghton College, at the direction of its president, Daniel R. Chamberlain, began a quiet search for an appropriate location in the city of Buffalo where it might develop an urban extension site. In December of 1987 the college became aware of efforts to save an architecturally and historically significant church building in the inner city, which had been marked for demolition, and joined the struggle to save it. A July 9, 1988, editorial in *The Buffalo News* noted Houghton's effort as follows: "THE BEAUTIFUL and historic St. Mary of Sorrows Church, towering over a depressed area of Buffalo's East Side, is too precious to both its neighborhood and the city to be lost to demolition. Now, to the community's credit, signs are good that it won't be. . . . . Important support is being offered by Houghton College, an Allegany County liberal arts institution that is making its presence more strongly felt in the Buffalo area. . . . . Its participation is a welcome boost to the efforts to save this landmark."

In the fall of 1988 Charles E. Massey, a professor of education at Houghton, joined the board of the Sacred Sites Restoration Corporation (renamed the King Urban Life Center, Inc.) which was formed to oversee restoration of the building for secular use. In 1989 he and Stephen C. Halpern, a fellow board member and a political science professor at the University at Buffalo, approached the presidents of the 20 institutions in the Western New York Consortium of Higher Education to request that they establish a Committee On Inner City Initiatives to work with the King Urban Life Center (King Center). In February 1990 the presidents voted unanimously to form the Committee and charged it to explore how the talent of the higher education community could be brought to bear to address some of the concerns of citizens on Buffalo's East Side—the city's largely African American inner city community.

In the fall of 1991, through the efforts of the Committee On Inner City Initiatives and under the leadership of Halpern and Massey, a group of educators began to meet informally to discuss educational needs in the King Center community. The gathering included the Dean of the Graduate School of Education at the University of Buffalo, the Director of Curriculum for the Buffalo Public Schools, the recently retired Associate Superintendent of the Buffalo Public Schools, faculty from three area colleges, members of the Buffalo Board of Education, and the King Center board. After nearly a year of almost weekly meetings, the HoJo's Group (so called because its 7:00 a.m. meetings were at a Howard Johnson's Restaurant in Buffalo) agreed that a model early childhood school should be considered as the anchor for the King Center. The group recommended that a more comprehensive study of the possibility be made during the 1992-93 academic year.

In September 1992, a study team—including educators in the fields of early childhood, social work and nursing, a public school administrator, directors of a coalition of home day care providers, and a trustee of a major Buffalo foundation—began a comprehensive study of the King Center community and the needs of its young children. Meeting biweekly at Buffalo Public School #90, an early childhood center serving 800 prekindergarten through second grade children, the study team produced a concept paper to guide the development of the King Center school and recommended that the King Center initiate a pilot project at School #90.

The study team concluded that the King Center should be "a national prototype program" in which the higher education community of Western New York, in partnership with leaders of Buffalo's East Side, develops a community center and early childhood school "devoted to serving the needs of children and families." The King Center should provide comprehensive services to support families, making the care and education of children from birth to eight years of age the focal point of its work. It should be founded on the idea that ". . . in providing for and educating children we must involve, support and care for the entire family." Consequently, the King Center should offer comprehensive services to support and nurture healthy, strong families. The school, as envisioned by the study team, would "provide an environment rich in computers and other high technology educational tools to help children learn and teachers teach." It would "be founded on the idea of developing individualized learning programs for each child." The school would serve approximately 100 students in prekindergarten through third grade.

In September of 1993 the King Center initiated a pilot program in Buffalo Public School #90, one of the city's largest early childhood centers serving inner city children from three to seven years of age.

The Electronic Portfolio

Claity Price Massey, professor of early childhood education at Houghton College and a member of the King Center study team, and Darlene G. Bressler, professor of elementary education at Houghton, had been impressed with the potential to use portfolio assessment to collect and organize information about a child's academic and non-academic performance and employ those data to continually evaluate the child's development and determine an individualized instructional program for the child. They were also aware that a teacher's capacity to collect, organize and evaluate such data for an entire class was limited. However, advances in computer technologies, especially multimedia, suggested that the development of "electronic portfolios" might provide an answer to this dilemma. During the 1992-1993 academic year, Massey used a part of her sabbatical at Houghton to evaluate the computer-based portfolio programs on the market and under development, with the intention of choosing the most promising one for use in the King Center school pilot, planned to begin in the fall of 1993 at Buffalo Public School #90.

Her search took her to Manchester, Vermont to see the work of two public school teachers, Doug Snow and Bob Densmore, whose pioneering effort to develop an electronic portfolio had caught the attention of Apple

Computers and Scholastic. Massey's interest resulted in an invitation to participate with the development team being assembled by Scholastic. In the spring of 1993 School #90 became one of a half-dozen testing sites for the beta testing of the electronic portfolio. It was the only inner city site, and the only site to continue working with the portfolio prototype while the final product was in development. Massey's work led to a consulting role during the spring and summer of 1994 and eventuated with her serving as the lead author for the Scholastic Electronic Portfolio which was marketed in March of 1995. Her involvement with multimedia also enabled Houghton College to enhance its reputation as a leader in the use of educational technology.

Prior Use of Educational Technology at Houghton

During the 1980's and early 1990's, Houghton College established itself at the forefront in New York State in the use of technology for educational innovation. It was first recognized by the State Education Department in 1984 for development of a fully interactive two-way microwave communication system linking its rural and suburban campuses, some fifty-five miles apart. During the 1986-87 academic year the college worked with the Erie I Board of Cooperative Educational Services (BOCES) in the development of a distance education system utilizing computers, phones and Optel audiographic software. Constance R. Finney, a Houghton education professor, taught the Advanced Placement calculus course which inaugurated the system by linking 22 students at nine schools (rural, suburban and urban). Between 1988 and 1990, under the direction of Willis Beardsley, co-director of the college's Center for Technology in Education, pilot distance education projects were carried out with Buffalo City Schools, Wheatland-Chili High School, Pioneer Middle School and Fillmore Central School. Over the past five years the college has established Optel-based distance education programs linking Houghton to Parents for Quality Education at the Langston Hughes Institute in Buffalo, New York; Wesleyan Academy in Puerto Rico; and Hong Kong Baptist College.

Thirteen years ago the college became involved with educational technology in an effort to address barriers between its campuses. Today the technology is also being used to address racial, cultural and socioeconomic barriers. Teacher education students in rural Houghton, New York, interact regularly with inner city elementary school children (mostly African American) at the Langston Hughes Institute in Buffalo. Students in the "Puerto Rico: Language, Culture and Society" course have conversed with high school students at Wesleyan Academy in Guaynabo, Puerto Rico. Teacher education students in the "Tutoring and Teaching With Technology" course at Houghton have been linked with students at Hong Kong Baptist College to compare their cultures and college experiences. However, it was not until the fall of 1993 that the college was able to establish a state-of-the-art multimedia laboratory for its teacher education program.

The Houghton Multimedia Lab

Building on Claity Price Massey's work during her 1992-93 sabbatical, the college approached the NYNEX Foundation and the Margaret L. Wendt Foundation in the spring of 1993, proposing that they "form a partnering relationship to provide financial support for establishing and staffing a multimedia lab to enhance the work of the Houghton College teacher education program." The Wendt Foundation responded with a $50,000 grant for equipment and NYNEX provided $87,000 over two years for staff and operations. A Macintosh-based multimedia laboratory was installed in August of 1993. With a $20,000 grant from an anonymous Buffalo foundation, the lab was upgraded in August of 1994. The creation of this multimedia lab enables Houghton College to prepare both preservice and inservice teachers for the technology-based schools of today and tomorrow.

Teacher Education

The Houghton College teacher education program provides courses for preservice teachers and institutes and workshops for inservice teachers. Participants in any of these programs will examine the use of multimedia as a presentation tool to enhance teacher classroom presentations as well as a tool to put into the hands of students for cooperative and individual project work and presentations. CD ROM and videodisc programs are demonstrated for and explored by participants. Multimedia for portfolio development and authentic assessment is also investigated.

Multimedia tools participants learn to use include a Power Macintosh computer, scanner, digital camera, audio input and video input and output devices. Through hands-on experiences they are introduced to the Scholastic Electronic Portfolio software and use this program to create personal portfolios. A Kodak CD Writer is then used to permanently record the portfolios for the participants. The multimedia dimensions of telecommunications are experienced through personal use of the Internet utilizing Netscape.

Programs are tailored to meet the needs of individual participants, from technology novices to experts. During the summers of 1994 and 1995 teachers and administrators from Buffalo Public School #90 and the King Center School pilot were among those utilizing the multimedia lab.

The King Center School Pilot

Now in its third year, the King Center School pilot at School #90 serves 70 four- to six-year-old children, including ten special needs children in an inclusion program. Housed in three classrooms, the pilot is staffed by three classroom teachers, an inclusion teacher and three aides. Four interns from the Graduate School of Social Work at the University of Buffalo and two student teachers from Houghton College are also working with the pilot this year. This pilot is providing data and an experiential base from which to develop the programs to be implemented at the King Center when the restoration and renovation of the former St. Mary of Sorrows Church building is completed in the fall of 1997.

A school-linked community health care center is currently under development. Located three blocks from School #90 and directly across the street from the King Center facility, the King Center-Geneva B. Scruggs Health Care Pilot will be housed in a former "crack" house. Funded through a $225,000 grant from Independent Health Foundation, the Health Care Pilot will begin providing care for children in the King Center School pilot and their families, in January of 1996. The Health Care Pilot will also serve as a test site for an Electronic Health Care Portfolio under development by Children's Hospital of Buffalo.

During its first year and a half, the King Center School Pilot was lead by Claity Price Massey of Houghton College with the assistance of David Day, Chairman of the Elementary Education and Reading Department at Buffalo State College and James Hoot, Director of the Early Childhood Research Center at the University of Buffalo, all working as volunteers. In the spring of 1994, Charles Massey began work on a plan to raise the funds needed to aggressively move the Pilot forward. With the assistance of other members of the King Urban Life Center Board, this effort produced six grants totaling $278,000 by the spring of 1995.

The Institute for Applied Urban Educational Research

The Institute for Applied Urban Educational Research (IAUER) was established by the King Urban Life Center Board in the fall of 1994 "to coordinate and oversee all educational programs and to continue to initiate and promote innovative and state-of-the-art applications for early education." In January of 1995 the Board named Claity Price Massey the first Director of IAUER, after negotiating with Houghton College for a portion of her time.

In its work with the School #90 Pilot, IAUER is attempting to identify barriers preventing four-, five- and six-year-old inner city public school children from achieving success in school and exploring how these barriers might be overcome. At present Massey is giving special attention to the need to provide a truly individualized educational program for each child and the use of an electronic portfolio as a tool to assist teachers in this endeavor. David Day, working with graduate students at Buffalo State College, has begun a "Child-Environment Interaction" research project designed to obtain data regarding the naturalistic behavior of children in two of the King Center Pilot classrooms. These data will be of value in assessing the contribution of the curriculum to the development and learning of all of the children and will be useful to the teachers as they continue to build an effective curriculum.

When the King Urban Life Center moves into the former St. Mary of Sorrows Church building in the fall of 1997, it will become the permanent home of IAUER and the King Center School. This model demonstration early childhood school and research institute will serve as a resource for teacher education in Buffalo and throughout the country. In the meantime, the King Center School Pilot and Houghton College are proving that true school/college collaboration can make everyone a winner.

Inservice Teacher Education

Clintonia Graves is an extraordinary teacher who is learning to use computer-based technology as a tool in teaching. But this didn't come easily. When she began the 1994-95 school year as teacher of a multi-age classroom for children four and five years old, with the King Center Pilot at School #90, she had had little exposure to computers and none to multimedia. She did, however, bring enthusiasm and determination— two ingredients that have served her well.

A day-long inservice workshop in the multimedia laboratory at Houghton College in August of 1994 was followed by individualized on-site instruction at School #90 during the early fall. The workshop and on-site instruction were given by Claity Price Massey and Nathan Danner, computer technical assistant at Houghton. Graves learned quickly and by November was beginning the development of individual student's portfolios, including pictures of the children taken with a digital camera, scans of their art work and audio clips of them introducing themselves. But it was the arrival of Macintoshes for the children and a PowerBook for the teacher that opened up new vistas for Graves. Thanks to a grant from the Margaret L. Wendt Foundation and the Buffalo State College Research Foundation, the teachers' work with the technology was no longer confined to the hours when the school was open and the children could have daily hands-on experience with computers.

By January of 1995, Graves, with fellow teacher Janine Felckowski and Pilot Director Claity Price Massey, was ready to give a live demonstration of the electronic portfolio at a meeting of the Buffalo Board of Education. The meeting was videotaped and aired the following Saturday on public access television.

When Graves and Felckowski decided to use the four Macintoshes in each of their classrooms to run WiggleWorks, a beginning literacy program from Scholastic, they visited with first grade teachers who were already using the program with their children. The first grade teachers were willing instructors for Graves and Felckowski, but their cooperation went one wonderful step further—they sent some of their computer literate first graders to teach the prekindergartners and kindergartners how to use the computers. This peer teaching has been a great success.

James is a five year-old in Graves' class whose language development has progressed very slowly. She had noticed that he spoke only one or two words at a time and he recognized no words in print. She had tried a variety of ways to assist him, to no avail. One day in February she noticed James singing a simple song he had learned in class. She sat James in front of a computer and asked him to sing the song again. When he did, she recorded it as an entry in his portfolio. When he had finished, she played it back for him to hear. He listened closely, then said, "That's me singing!" Over the next several weeks he asked repeatedly to hear himself sing on the computer. During this time Graves was working with James on the identification of words. When he could identify these words, she put them into a sentence and entered the words into the electronic portfolio program, then recorded James saying the words as they appeared on the computer screen. James listened carefully as she played it back, then responded with a sense of awe, "I can read!"

Computer technology is not a magic cure for all of our educational woes, but in the hands of a capable, creative, caring teacher, such as Clintonia Graves, it can become a powerful tool for learning. Recognizing this, Massey and Danner take great pride in the success of Graves and the children in her classroom and the role they have played in supporting her efforts. They have also recognized her potential as a model for aspiring teachers in the college's preservice teacher education program.

Preservice Teacher Education

In September of 1995, David Robbins began his student teaching semester at Houghton College. As part of a teacher education program pilot, he will spend the entire fall semester in Clintonia Graves' multi-age classroom. Claity Price Massey serves as the Houghton College Supervisor for his student teaching experience and Nathan Danner continues to provide limited technical support. Thursday (September 21, 1995) Mrs. Graves and some of the children in the class played "show and tell" with a group of 20 visitors from Japan, demonstrating the Electronic Portfolio and WiggleWorks, while Mr. Robbins worked with the other children in the class. Mrs. Massey heard all about it from Mrs. Graves during the King Center School Pilot Leadership Team meeting at School #90 the following day.

Writing for the Houghton College education department in the spring of 1995, Charles Massey stated: "Teacher education courses taught in isolation on college or university campuses have little impact on the kind of teachers these institutions produce. The most significant factor in the professional development of teachers is the student teaching experience." In light of this, the teacher education program pilot is attempting to establish the school classroom teacher, the student teacher and the college supervisor as a team, working together to provide the best possible learning situation for each child, while the classroom teacher and college supervisor work together to direct and nurture the student teacher.

While it is too soon to draw many conclusions, the early results indicate that everyone may come out a winner!

Conclusion

After eight years of pursuing solutions to its geographic and cultural isolation, Houghton College remains a rural college (sixty five miles from Buffalo) with a very homogeneous population. However, its partnership with the King Urban Life Center and its leadership in the Pilot at School #90 are reducing its isolation and continuing to make new friends.

The Professional Education Model as a Catalyst for Reform And Renewal of a School-Based Program

Kathleen M. Manning
Gerald W. Jorgenson

John Carroll University (Ohio)

Historically, there have been ongoing questions as to how people learn. Our systems of education have examined these various "philosophies" and from them have developed organized bodies of education labeled "school." Potential sources of influence have included those who believed knowledge was innate; those who believed knowledge was based on experiences; or, those who believed in the innate concept, but placed the necessity of experience and readiness as key factors. Additional influences come from behavioral psychologists concerned with conditioning and measuring of behavior; and developmental theorists like Piaget and Vygotsky who found the concept of knowledge and process of learning to be quite compound and complex.

These varied thoughts on effective learning have influenced beliefs about what makes effective teaching, and what constitutes effective teacher education preparation. The ideal would be that learning, teaching, and teacher education preparation would be highly interrelated. But the literature sends a different message: teacher preparation does not seem to be effective within the present model, i.e., the University teacher education program and public/private school education seem to be separate entities. This concern has instigated a process of reform in teacher education as to alternate ways to achieve an inclusive teacher education model. The current most popular suggestion seems to be the Professional Development School (PDS). "PDSs aim to provide new models of teacher education and development by serving as exemplars of practice, builders of knowledge, and vehicles for communicating professional understanding among teacher educators, novices, and veteran teachers" (Darling-Hammond, 1994, p. 1).

The question of the PDS as an effective instrument for reform and renewal has created much debate, and initiated programs with variations of the same model, as well as completely different conceptual models. Research literature on the PDSs identifies significant work on philosophy, quality of partnerships, funding, outcomes, successes/failures, and individual case studies. A central point is to explain how the PDS model can initiate, or become the catalyst for, renewal and reform of teacher education programs, specifically, and the whole system of education in general (Darling-Hammond, 1994, Robinson and Darling-Hammond, 1994, Teitel, 1994).

This paper will describe one version of the PDS, a School-Based partnership, between a small liberal arts university and selected school programs throughout Greater Cleveland. The intention is to provide a case history of successful partnerships by sharing a "working, developmental model" for professional teacher education.

Partnerships
John Carroll University

John Carroll is a coeducational, Jesuit, liberal arts college in University Heights, Ohio, comprised of a College of Arts & Sciences, and a Graduate and Business School. There are approximately 4,400 full time and part time undergraduate and graduate students, with the traditional undergraduate student as the primary population. The original John Carroll School-Based partnership began in 1981.

South Euclid-Lyndhurst School District

South Euclid-Lyndhurst is a traditional, public, culturally diverse school district with approximately 4,000 students, K-12. This district has been partners within the School-Based program since 1987 when the Superintendent of South Euclid-Lyndhurst and a Professor of Education at John Carroll University, ". . . conceived of a bold and ambitious project," with a two-fold purpose: ". . . to attract highly trained, caring individuals" to educate future generations, and provide an opportunity to the ". . . talented veteran teachers . . . mid-career opportunities for professional development and career advancement" (Weaver, Weaver and Franko, 1992, p. 652). The original School-Based program, which had begun in 1981, was confined to a private boys' school; the addition of South Euclid-Lyndhurst provided an opportunity for diversity in professional teacher education for the School-Based interns. Intern placement in South Euclid-Lyndhurst for the 1995-96 academic year includes 3 lower elementary schools, 1 upper elementary school, 1 junior high school and 1 high school.

These additional sites were added for the 1995-1996 school year.

Orchard Elementary School

Orchard Elementary School is part of the Cleveland Public School District. Orchard accommodates approximately 615 students K-5, bussed from thirteen (13) neighborhoods throughout Cleveland. Orchard is a science magnet school which accounts for the eclectic student body.

Hawken Lower School

Hawken Lower School is an independent, coeducational day school, with 497 students preschool through 8th grade. The students select to attend Hawken from throughout the Greater Cleveland area.

St. Ignatius High School

St. Ignatius High School is a Jesuit, Catholic, private boys' college preparatory high school, with an enrollment of 1,350 students. Students attend from throughout the Greater Cleveland area, with acceptance dependent upon grades, recommendations, and entrance exam scores

Philosophy

The School-Based concept has a 14-year tradition at John Carroll University, primarily built upon long-standing personal and professional relationships between faculty at the University and Teacher Education sites. The premise was one of mutual respect and mutual belief in the efficacy of site-based preparation of professional educators. In effect, John Carroll University has had in place for a decade and a half a version of the Professional Development Schools now being discussed and formed throughout the United States. What is interesting about the John Carroll program is that the developmental characteristics of a proposed program as discussed by Darling-Hammond (1994) can be seen in the evolution of our program throughout these 14 years. Our original School-Based relationships were as Darling-Hammond (1994) states, ". . . those that got off to the most propitious starts are the ones that grew out of preexisting personal and organizational relationships. . . . had engaged people in collaborative work around a variety of shared goals over a period of time" (p. 21). This statement is a summary of the John Carroll program.

During 1994-95, John Carroll extended an invitation to certain potential new sites to join this professional education partnership to provide a greater diversity of intern opportunities. Whereas the South Euclid-Lyndhurst partnership was conceived by professional peers tacitly accepting a common philosophy and mission, these new alliances were presented with the John Carroll philosophy and mission as these were defined within our NCATE model (Figure 1). The new professional

Figure 1

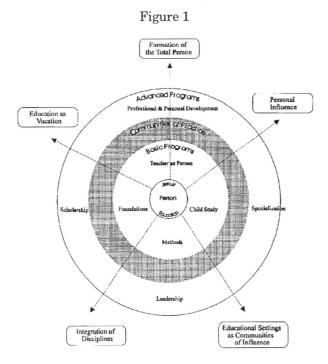

partnerships thus were formed through a discussion of a clear university philosophy, mission, and purpose, and allowed the potential sites to join John Carroll in the professional development of teachers.

Thus the early history of our successful long-standing program with South Euclid-Lyndhurst was first achieved through an informal process which assumed a shared vision. Subsequent partnerships were established through a more formal process with the same vision involving collaboration, cooperation and mutual respect for everyone's role within the professional partnership, but the new partnership did so from the perspective of clear philosophical and programmatic guidelines. All partners were thus able to reflect on their own philosophy and mission as they relate to the common goal of preparing teachers who are reflective, critical, flexible, and thoughtful in their profession.

Program Description

The School-Based program, developed in 1981, is an Ohio Board of Regents approved alternative teacher certification program. The interns accepted into this program receive a Master's of Education degree as well as elementary or secondary teacher certification depending on their academic background. The essential details of this teacher certification and Master's degree program have not been altered over time.

The academic program consists of 40 semester hours of coursework distributed between various school sites and the University. The coursework begins in June at John Carroll and continues through the May or August Commencement. The program is University-based during the summer and becomes site-based with the Fall semester. The interns report to their teaching assignments and begin an academic year of immersion in the dynamics of professional education in concert with a mentor teacher with whom each intern is paired for the academic year. Throughout the academic year, time is divided between being a teacher/ facilitator within the classroom, attending classes on site, and attending evening classes at the University. The individual sites provide faculty who, at the site, teach methods, encourage professional development, and supervise student teaching. The University provides faculty for the graduate courses held at John Carroll.

An additional aspect of this partnership concerns the financial arrangements for this program. The School-Based program is self-supporting through tuition. The School-Based sites receive a portion of the tuition for courses taken on-site from which program costs, professional development activities for faculty, and salaries are deducted. This arrangement provides the impetus for professional development of veteran teachers. Sites have financial discretion for use of this income in ways that benefit faculty, interns, and the school as a whole.

Admission

The School-Based program is available to individuals who have a Bachelor of Arts or Sciences degree with a strong liberal arts background. The applicants must: (a) have a strong liberal arts background; (b) meet graduate school requirements for a Master's of Education degree; (c) be capable of achieving teacher certification; and (d) be accepted for an internship at a partner school.

The selection of potential interns requires the professional involvement of both University personnel and the representatives from specific school sites. John Carroll assumes responsibility for the initial evaluation of previous academic preparation and performance, professional intent, and potential candidacy for a Master's degree and teacher certification. The next layer of evaluation which becomes the "heart" of the program is the site evaluation of interns. Official acceptance of an intern into the School-Based program depends upon formal acceptance by a site. This is the critical step which "drives" the success and quality of an intern's experiences throughout the year-long immersion into the culture of the elementary or secondary teaching experiences. The value of the intern sites is reflected in Darling-Hammond's (1994) statement about the PDS, to "provide the thoughtful introduction to practice needed to enable teachers to make informed judgments in complex situations with the support of colleagues in a reflective, knowledge-rich environment" (p.6).

NCATE Model

The School-Based program has evolved, and matured over time, but still has been faithful to the original shared goal, the preparation and development of professional educators. The catalyst for revisiting the school-based program was the development of the John Carroll Department of Education's professional education model for NCATE accreditation. STANDARD I.A: Design of Curriculum deals with the development of a model ". . . that explicates the purposes, processes, outcomes, and evaluation of the program. . . . and the knowledge bases that undergird[s] them . . ." (NCATE Standards, 1990, p. 45)

Department of Education faculty researched this standard for two years in an effort to clearly frame the University's and Department's philosophy and mission statements in the context of tradition, theory, research, and professional practice. Out of this process emerged a "model" for the program, which

> . . . attempts to illustrate the organic nature of professional education in the Department's basic and advanced programs. Although depicted as a series of concentric circles embedded one within another, development of the total person as an educator expands in a spiral fashion in relation to the strands through interactions with program curricula and communities of educational practice. (NCATE Report, 1994, p. 1-8)

The visual depiction of the model (figure 1) was new; the philosophy of the model, however, was not new, because the Department of Education had already been living and practicing within the guides of this model without an overt acknowledgment of such. The model thus became the symbol for the John Carroll University standards of Professional Teacher Education, philosophy, mission and program, including the School-Based program.

The model gave a point for reflection about this program, and an opportunity for renewal. Philosophically, the program literally embodied the five characteristics of the Jesuit ideal of an educator, which are demonstrated in the model as "spokes" emanating from the very core of our program, the person. The selection of interns stresses the personal, professional and individualistic qualities of each person. The program strives for mature adults with diverse educational and employment experiences.

The unique nature of the School-Based program finds an overlap with the four strands for the Basic Program, and the four strands for the Advanced Program. The yearlong immersion within a school site, the 40 semester hours of graduate coursework, and the personal mentoring approach to the interns dictate a cohesive, educational, reflective learning environment.

Beyond these time-honored success points, the question was raised about the full impact of the collaborative process. Were we operating as two distinct programs: theory and practical application? This was the strength of the inclusive NCATE model. The program did not change, nor did the partnership model under which we had developed the program. What began to change was the interaction of the two programs: the elimination of discrete programs, and the development of a process of collaboration in a true form. A process of communication and collaboration commenced through John Carroll's Department of Education in the development of an integrated relationship between the University and the School-Based sites. This relationship would gradually move the School-Based program from the fringe of the University to the core of the University, as the core was described in the NCATE model. Since the program was successful, the concern for change was quite obvious; but the underlying factor was to take the spirit of the model, explain the professional development of our students as teacher educators, and provide a forum through which each individual school-based site could explore and enhance its own personal and program professional development. This also provided the challenge for the school-based sites to enhance their own philosophy and mission statement as institutions of learning, in concert with that of John Carroll.

South Euclid-Lyndhurst held meetings with the Department of Education School-Based administrators throughout the summer of 1994, for strategic planning. Two priorities were identified: communication and collaboration, a focus on the NCATE model that served as an over- arching umbrella common to the University and public school sites. Strategic planning, flowing from a common philosophy, thus in a natural way ensured that the school site was at the core, rather than the fringe, of the University. Thus we could collaborate, communicate, disagree, and grow.

Strengths of Change

One task for the partnership was to strengthen the University-School collaborative process. Immediate actions were simple and obvious for a "real" partnership: faculty parking permits, library privileges, access to recreational facilities for School-Based faculty. These were acknowledgments of professional association with the University rather than visitor status.

The interns' role in the John Carroll community was also addressed. The interns previously attended graduate classes at the University, but their physical identification was with the school site. During the academic year 1994-95, the interns were perceived as John Carroll graduate students, not as a discrete entity, with the same privileges and services as all graduate students. Faculty involvement was increased within the program, primarily through the addition of a faculty member as program administrator, and the use of full-time faculty advisers for the interns. Summer orientation sessions were held with the Graduate Dean, Financial Aid Adviser, Bookstore Manager, Recreation Director, and others to provide specific information in their area. Program books were compiled to provide a handy reference for important information, including a very thorough academic calendar. As a result of requests from interns, a Professional Development workshop was held the first year on Classroom Behavior and Management, and three have been scheduled for the 1995-96 year, with the additional topics of Ethics in Teaching and Assessment. Financial Aid counseling was increased for the academic year. The services of the Business Office to provide financial assistance in securing loans were also increased. Other services for the interns included availability of faculty for conversations, the services of the career advisement office, and participation within the employment network available to all education students.

Concerns from Change

No change occurs without some problems or concerns. The following are examples of potential sources which could create problems for a School-Based program. The most obvious concern with these changes has been the increased demands of faculty time and secretarial resources. The applicant pool for the School-Based interns tends to be quite diverse, and therefore significant time is required for transcript evaluations, interviews, discussions as to capability of success, and ongoing support throughout the intense year. A full-time secretary is necessary as a contact person for these students. Also, full-time faculty find an increase in time requirements for student advising. For true collaboration, meetings that provide opportunities for sharing must occur on a regular basis. And the desire to make quick administrative decisions must be curtailed, because decision-making in a collaborative relationship is necessarily slower.

Summary

Throughout this document, a descriptive process has been presented of a program established upon a foundation of friendship with mutual respect for quality teacher preparation. Throughout the 14-year process, successes and challenges have been encountered, with strong long term results. The School-Based interns have been able to fulfill a desire to become a professional educator; the University has been involved in a cooperative teacher education program with fine academic programs; the interns have found employment upon completion of the program; and the program has been financially successful for the cooperating programs, which in turn supported professional development of veteran teachers. Additional changes may and will be needed, but the ability to judge the purpose, value and necessity will be tempered by our NCATE model, a model of our past, a view of our present, and a reflection of our future.

References

Darling-Hammond, L. (1994). Developing professional development schools: early lessons, challenge, and promise. In L. Darling-Hammond, Ed., *Professional development schools: Schools for developing a profession*. New York: Teachers College Press.

Department of Education, John Carroll University. (1994). Institutional Report. (Publication prepared for NCATE accreditation). University Heights, OH.

National Council for the Accreditation of Teacher Education (NCATE). (1990). NCATE Standards, Procedures, and Policies for the Accreditation of Professional Standards. Washington, D.C.

Robinson, S. P. and Darling-Hammond, L. (1994) Change for collaboration and collaboration for change: Transforming teaching through school-university partnerships. in L. Darling-Hammond, Ed., *Professional development schools: Schools for developing a profession*. New York: Teachers College Press.

Teitel, L. (1994). Can school-university partnerships lead to the simultaneous renewal of schools and teacher education? *Journal of Teacher Education, 45* (4), 245-252.

Weaver, C. C., Weaver, S. L., Franko, S. (1992). Teacher education and staff development: A win-win combination. *Phi Delta Kappan. 73* (8), 652 & 654.

The Kentucky Wesleyan College And Cravens Elementary School Partnership: A Work In Process

Jo M. Tennison
Janice Hawes

Kentucky Wesleyan College

> "I didn't realize how much I had missed before I began to work collaboratively. Once you collaborate, you never want to go back!" A Cravens Elementary School teacher

Introduction

Kentucky Wesleyan College (KWC) and Cravens Elementary School have developed an effective educational partnership committed to the preparation of preservice teachers. This collaboration did not begin with a finely tuned plan, but instead developed over time with ideas and input from the teachers and students at both institutions. The partnership's success is revealed by the belief that all of the partners feel they gain immensely from this partnership.

In The Beginning

Nearly seven years ago, Kentucky Wesleyan College's President, Paul Hartman, visited Cravens Elementary School while looking for ways in which college students could bring service leadership into the community. In return, Cravens school representatives visited a college faculty meeting to explore possibilities of KWC students becoming involved in service learning at Cravens. While a few departments expressed mild interest, the Teacher Education Department faculty began to work closely with the Cravens administration and faculty to examine the needs of both parties and determine how each could serve the other.

At this time, the Teacher Education faculty was redesigning the Teacher Education program and the new program required field experiences as a part of every professional education class. The faculty desired a close link with public schools to provide laboratory experiences for their education students with children in authentic environments. The KWC faculty knew the Cravens environment would provide for their education students real-world learning, with the ambiguity, unpredictability and honesty that children bring to learning; they also believed that their education students would stimulate new experiences of learning for the Cravens children and faculty.

The Participants and the Setting

Kentucky Wesleyan College was moved from eastern Kentucky to Owensboro in 1951. As a small, private, liberal arts college, Kentucky Wesleyan serves a predominately white student population of 700, with approximately 130 of those students enrolled in the Teacher Education program. Most of the students are from Kentucky and the surrounding states, but some do come from more distant states and from foreign countries. The Teacher Education Department is staffed by three full-time and two part-time faculty, all of whom have more than 20 years teaching experience in public schools and in higher education. Four of the five have joined the Wesleyan faculty within the last five years.

Cravens Elementary School is a neighborhood school, one of six public elementary schools in the city of Owensboro. It serves a population of 350 pupils in pre-K through grade 4. About 40% of the Cravens children are minority children, more than 80% are eligible for free or reduced lunch, and the school qualifies for schoolwide Title 1 project. The neighborhood includes government subsidized housing units and single family homes. It faces additional stresses of violence, substance dealing and abuse, and unsafe living conditions. Nearly 25% of Cravens children have been involved with Social Services in issues of abuse or neglect in the last five years.

Nearly one third of Cravens parents are unemployed, while most of the remaining parents work part-time or in full-time minimum wage jobs. They are the working poor. One third of Cravens children live in families headed by a single parent, 38% live in traditional nuclear families, 23% live in blended families and 6% live with relatives. Although parental concern for their children's success at school is high, parental involvement is low because of conflicts with parents' work schedules and the need for child care.

In response to KERA, the Kentucky Education Reform Act of 1990, Cravens is organized into nongraded, multiage primary classes (K - 4).

All of the teachers are organized into teams of two or three teachers who plan together and then implement their instruction in a variety of ways. Most of Cravens teachers, 80%, have fewer than eight years of teaching experience, while 20% have more than ten years of teaching exprience. As practicing educators, they are managing reform initiatives, assuming new roles as mentors with KWC students, learning new skills, and working with new ideas.

The KWC Teacher Education Program

The KWC Teacher Education program prepares its students for Kentucky's three levels of certification: primary, K-4; middle grades, 5-8; and high school, 9-12.

The Teacher Education program is designed to include a conceptual framework of theory, a knowledge base in pedagogy, with clinical and field experiences. Every class in the program requires the education student to complete a specified number of hours of field experiences. These field experiences range from classroom observations required at all three levels for the "Introduction to Education" class, to gradually increasing levels of involvement with planning and teaching by the education student in the upper level classes. Teacher education students will have worked a minimum of 150 hours in the schools before they begin student teaching.

Teacher education students are empowered early in their educational program to identify their own learning needs. They learn to do so through the requirements of their classes, from working with children, and from striving to meet Kentucky's "New Teacher Standards." They become increasingly skilled at identifying and discussing their learning progress through self-evaluations of their experiences, through their reflective journals, and through the feedback from observations and evaluations made by their peers, by mentor teachers, and by college faculty.

Using all available information, the preservice teacher and professor discuss the student's learning needs in relation to the requirements the student must complete for each class, and jointly they identify field experiences appropriate to the student's professional development. When those field experiences are identified for each education student, the requests are given to the Cravens Site Coordinator, who individually matches each student's needs and schedule with a teacher who can provide the desired experiences.

Coming Together

Cravens faculty recognized the validity of on-site experiences for education students and discussed the advantages they would gain and what they could give to others. They anticipated the benefits their students would incur by having more people in the classroom. They reflected on the value of children developing relationships with adults, and they said, "Wouldn't it be great to have these college students in our classes as role models for our students?"

But collaboration was synonymous with change, and Principal Beverly McEnroe admitted, "We were a little bit afraid of it at first. Here we opened our building to students, and we had lots of teachers who had closed doors. No one knew their roles: the teachers didn't; the KWC students didn't; the partnership was an evolving process."

' The Cravens teachers reflected about the beginning of the partnership remembering that they had had a voice in making decisions about the partnership. "It wasn't stated to us that 'this is the program KWC wants'; that would have been a lot more threatening. Instead, everyone saw this collaboration emerge; it was a learning experience for us." It was essential that everyone involved in the partnership had an equal voice in the creation of their roles and in the development of the partnership.

The single most critical element in the development and establishment of roles was identifying the needs of the KWC education students and making them accountable for satisfying their field experiences. When the education student was placed with a Cravens teacher, both student and teacher focused on a goal; their task was now identified, and both became responsible for satisfying that outcome.

From the beginning, Cravens teachers were allowed freedom to decide how they would respond to requests for field experiences from their Site Coordinator. Some teachers allowed student observations only. Some teachers immediately welcomed preservice teachers into their classrooms and put them to work listening to students read and assisting children in numerous ways. Most of the newer teachers were comfortable with college students in their classrooms because they had recently graduated from teacher education programs where they had been the college student who completed field experiences in the classroom. Several teachers admitted, "When the KWC students first came in, I was a little apprehensive and nervous that someone was watching me. I became much more aware of my planning. And then I realized that I had something to offer them. Now it is easier because they're so much a part of us."

Changes and Gains

Over time, Cravens teachers began to identify the rewards of accepting preservice teachers in their classrooms. One of the teachers reflected, and others agreed, that "my children like those KWC students and respond well for them. It's really nice to know that someone will walk through your door who can work with three of your students who need help with a specific skill; to be able to plan for that and have that done has been great."

The teachers noticed that their children adjusted easily to extra people in the room and were not distracted by KWC students coming and going. They noticed increasingly motivated children who consistently wanted to share their work with others. They noticed increased learning and skill development in their children. The children's self esteem blossomed from their positive experiences. The children also questioned the KWC students about why they were still in school when they were adults.

Tonishia, a seven-year-old Cravens student, was overheard reporting to her friend Stephanie as they walked down the hall, "I have a Wesleyan student." She spoke with real pride in her voice. Most students at Cravens felt they had a special KWC friend because KWC students were working in most of the classrooms in the building. All special needs children are included in regular classrooms at Cravens; there are no self-contained Special Education classrooms. The KWC students worked with all students and added their help to that already being given to special needs students. Special needs students no longer stood out among their peers. The school social worker noticed that parental interest in KWC students increased, and they began to request that a Wesleyan student work with their child. This change destigmatized children who needed special help.

The Cravens staff began to sense other changes in the school climate. More student work was displayed on the walls in the hallways because there were more hands to help display the work. Staff conversation changed from "my room" and "my children" to "our room" and "our children." "Years ago it was such a closed climate in the building," recalled Beverly McEnroe, "but now teachers share openly." One of the teachers stated, "If I don't know something, maybe someone else does; it is really helpful cooperating and working together."

Over time, the Cravens and the KWC faculties developed a high level of trust, allowing the professors to move comfortably into and out of classrooms at any time. When KWC students are teaching, a professor might ask to model some process or skill. This is done in a casual, participatory manner, and the children easily accept this since more than one teacher works with them much of the time. On such occasions, both the KWC student and the classroom teacher observe the teaching, and the children's participation with someone else.

Professors hold on-site discussions with their classes immediately following field expriences to help students reflect on and take meaning from their experiences. The Site Coordinator and the mentor teachers may join the discussions for multiple perspectives of the experiences. Teachers have identified as a problem their inability to leave their classrooms for discussions with the education students and the professors. To solve the problem, monies from a Goals 2000 grant have been designated for hiring floating substitutes, who will free the teachers from their classrooms for discussions.

Since Cravens teachers are not always available for conferences with education students and their professors, a special seminar is held each semester with the mentor teachers, and floating substitutes are hired to free the teachers to attend. Seminar discussions are designed to allow teachers to share their perspectives of the partnership, to examine problems, and to generate solutions.

The KWC Teacher Education faculty has seen the partnership become a strong unified effort to improve education for everyone involved. Working in the partnership has caused the KWC faculty to more carefully examine their curriculum and the alignment of their program. They have redesigned class curricula to link what students learn in each class and to progressively build on students' prior experiences. They have also eliminated the duplication of instruction by carefully examining class outcomes. The constant reality of working in Cravens classrooms has caused faculty members to teach fewer concepts in greater depth than they had previously. Students continually put into practice what they have discussed in the college classroom. They may discuss their experiences on-site or return to the college classroom after their experiences with Cravens children for discussions that help them construct their own knowledge about learning and teaching.

As teacher education students become more knowledgeable, they may observe teaching practice that does not fit their educational philosophies. When students are confronted by ideas and practices that are contrary to their beliefs, the disjunction causes them to question their own beliefs. This dialectical thinking process is the critical vehicle which allows them to construct their knowledge.

Patti, a senior education student, reflected on this process of constructing knowledge when she stated, "The practice I get in classrooms with children really helps me make sense of theory and process. When I can discuss my thoughts and experiences with others who have had different experiences, the learning is challenging. I can't leave a discrepancy alone. I either have to read more or initiate another experience with children until I arrive at the truth." It is this spirit of inquiry that results in the most significant learnings for students, and inquiry learnings are the most rewarding for the faculty members who assist in the process.

Special Events

Of the many collaborative experiences between KWC students and Cravens children, one of the children's favorites is the opportunity to watch their KWC friends play in a ball game. They may eat together in the dining hall and visit the dorm rooms. Education students want Cravens children to be exposed to college and to the idea that they could attend college, too.

Early in the partnership, two KWC Teacher Education faculty members and their students enrolled in methods and language arts classes, planned and implemented a Multicultural Fair at Cravens school to culminate a unit on World Cultures. The education students initiated and secured a Kentucky Education Association mini-grant to fund the fair. The fourth grade children at Cravens had been studying the cultures of India, Native Americans, and the Orient, and they had been involved in researching and writing about each culture. The physical education specialist had taught the children native dances and games of the various cultures. The Fair provided the children an opportunity to share what they had learned with the rest of the Cravens children and their families.

The fair was set up one day each week for three weeks. KWC education students set up centers in the gym representing the cultures of India on the first day, Native American cultures the second day, and Oriental cultures the third day. The children participated in storytelling with puppets they had made, dancing native dances, cooking native foods, wearing costumes they made, describing their art works and sharing genuine artifacts they had collected. The fourth graders also assisted other children with sand painting, creating spice booklets native to India, and playing native games.

The KWC education students planned the centers, implemented the activities, and managed the students who shared. The education students realized the Cravens teachers did not have the time, the help or the money required to create a culminating activity of such magnitude. Working together made the Multicultural Fair possible and provided an authentic learning experience for KWC students through collaboration with colleagues, children, teachers and staff.

One of Wesleyan's foreign students, Yoko, shared her Japanese culture with Cravens children through mini-lessons in their classrooms. She shared Japanese words and customs through role play activities, taught them to make dolls in Japanese dress and taught the art of origami to older children.

A special needs Cravens child taught Touch Math to the college students enrolled in the class "Mathematics for Elementary Teachers."

The experience boosted this student's self-esteem, which improved his attitude and his motivation to learn.

The KWC Teacher Education faculty secured a Campus Serve grant, awarded to provide service learning for preservice teachers, that stimulated another idea in KWC education students. They determined that a reading loft built at Cravens would be great fun for the children and would stimulate them to read. One of the education students, John, had carpentry experience, so he drew the scale plan for the loft. He secured approval from the Cravens' administration and faculty, and they determined the best site for the loft. John checked OSHA safety standards for the proper lumber to be used, traversed the school district regulations, and, with the help of the school custodian, built the loft in the library. Parents provided large pillows and bean bags for comfort. Cravens children prize this reading loft.

The KWC faculty used Goals 2000 grant money and hired a consultant to conduct a workshop at Cravens on the many ways to involve parents with their schools. Cravens parents, PTO members, staff and administration, as well as the KWC faculty and education students participated in the workshop. PTO members are discussing ways to provide opportunities for parents to serve by doing school work in their homes. As an example, two parents volunteered to cut out paper ladybugs at home for a classroom display at school.

The Cravens faculty transformed a former special education classroom into a science lab which was made available for use to all teachers. Dr. Coxon, a KWC professor, saw the opportunity to adjust her curriculum to involve her "Science and Math Methods" students in the establishment of the lab. Principal Beverly McEnroe, stated, "Dr. Coxon is going to bring her science students to work with our children, and we can watch the developmental process, while our children reap the rewards. It's a win-win situation no matter how you look at it."

The education students gathered science equipment from around the building, organized it in the lab, and made it operational. The methods students use the lab one morning a week to teach integrated science and math lessons, which they plan individually, to small groups of Cravens children. It provides the classroom teacher with the opportunity to observe methodologies and his/her children learning in another setting. Dr. Coxon and the education students discuss their experiences on site after the students have completed their teaching. Occasionally the students videotape their teaching for later analysis and reflection.

In addition, teacher education students interact with Cravens children in more individual ways. They share time and conversation with children over lunch, talk with children about how important education is for them, lead the 15-minute morning assembly for all Cravens students in the gym, bring the KWC basketball team to Cravens to tell the children how important reading is, teach and assist in the computer labs, assist children in gathering specimens from the outdoor science center, display children's work, staff learning centers in classrooms, listen to children read, and assist with children's writing.

While success is measured differently by each participant in this partnership, all believe they gain immensely from the partnership. KWC education students consistently rate their Cravens' experiences as the most valuable in their program. KWC faculty appreciate the depth of teaching that it affords them and the quality of learning it affords their students. Cravens teachers have taken on new responsibilities as mentors to KWC students and learn from them. Cravens students receive more individualized teaching from KWC students than they would without their help. Cravens children have scored significantly higher on statewide testing in recent years.

The Essentials

In our experience, the following guiding principles and components are essential if our partnership is to function efficiently.

1. A Home Base at the school where students check in, records are kept and messages may be left.

2. A Site Coordinator who works at the school and knows all of the teachers.

3. Support of the school administration, from the site level to the central office.

4. Equal voices of all participants in the continual design of the partnership.

5. A process for developing teachers' understandings of education students' assignments and philosophies of learning.

6. Student accountability for sincere efforts in the school and completion of the assigned tasks.

7. Constant communications between the members of the partnership.

8. Respect for each person's domain and individual style.

9. TIME; time to become comfortable with each other, to trust and to share.

We will continue to grow together to develop the partnership into a professional development site. There are problem areas that we are addressing. We have secured grants to help get our model in place. We will continue to grow without additional funds through the continuing collaboration of all constituents in the partnership.

Pre-Service Education in a Community of Practice: Site-based Secondary Methods

Keith Campbell
Frederic D. Ross

Linfield College (Oregon)

Introduction

The task of preparing college students for acculturation into the complex and daunting role of public school teachers presents problems which most teacher education faculty members recognize but for which few have easy solutions. Academic knowledge, management skills, lesson planning, and presentation skills are practiced and can even be perfected in college classrooms, but students don't really begin to take on the role of teacher in a traditional program until they are regularly in front of the classroom sometime during their student teaching. There is no planned, gradual transition from classroom practice to active participation in the new professional role: one minute they're students, the next they're teachers. Whatever happens during those first weeks of student teaching is often the result of accident, the effect of varying practices among cooperating teachers, school communities, and college faculty supervision practices.

We at Linfield addressed this problem directly several years ago when one seemingly well-prepared student teacher struggled to make that transition to the role of professional. During the 1991 spring semester Boyd Keyser, the social studies department chair at our local high school (McMinnville High School, hereafter MHS) who was also the cooperating teacher for a Linfield student teacher, and Keith Campbell, a new faculty member in secondary education and college supervisor for that student teacher, sat down one afternoon to discuss the student's tentative progress. Their conversation would become the impetus for dramatic changes in Linfield's secondary program.

Here was a student teacher with a solid academic background, who had demonstrated successful performance in the previous semester's secondary methods courses including several microteaching experiences, who had earned positive comments from a prior secondary aiding experience, who was conscientious, seemingly highly motivated, possessed of good social skills, and who was working under the tutelage of a masterful cooperating teacher who provided an excellent model and regular and specific feedback. Yet some eight weeks into his student teaching experience this model student was still floundering. Neither supervisor nor cooperating teacher could identify a particular instructional, planning, or management "skill" to focus on that was the crucial "weakness" that once addressed would result in a successful student teaching experience. The problem was more complex than lack of particular skills. It seemed more in the nature of an unusually prolonged inability to adapt to the culture of a high school classroom and the teacher's role in that culture.

The conversation progressed from a discussion of the dilemma of this particular student teacher to addressing these questions: How could all of us involved in the preparation of new teachers in both colleges of teacher education and public schools better acculturate preservice teachers to the realities of public school life prior to their student teaching experience? How could we ease the transition from college student to student teacher? How could we help students translate abstract theory into concrete practice? How could we expose students to the wisdom of practice earlier in their preparation? In other words, to frame these questions in light of Lave and Wenger's book *Situated Learning* (Lave & Wenger, 1991), what kinds of social engagements provide the proper context for learning to become an effective teacher and how can teacher education programs be structured to create such social engagements? Rather than asking what kinds of cognitive processes, conceptual structures, and specific planning, instructional, and management skills are required for effective teaching, or what sorts of student teacher placements Linfield students should have, we decided to look at the contexts of the teacher education program.

At the time of this conversation students seeking secondary teaching certification at Linfield enrolled in a methods block of eight semester credits taught by the authors. Students usually enrolled in these courses fall semester of their senior year following completion of nearly all of their major requirements and after completing six hours of educational foundations courses in their sophomore and junior years. All of these courses were taken on campus. The introductory foundations course had a 30-hour observation/aiding requirement usually in an elementary school; an additional course in exceptional children also required students to observe in schools. A 45-hour aiding requirement in a secondary classroom was required along with the methods block, although students took this course at various times. Any integration of methods coursework and field experience was haphazard and unplanned, and thus Linfield students would occasionally find themselves in the predicament described above: well prepared academically but unable to navigate the passage between college student and professional teacher.

Learning as Legitimate Peripheral Participation

Growing out of the tradition of social constructivism initiated by Soviet psychologists like Lev Vygotsky, Lave and Wenger (1991) argue for learning to be viewed as a situated activity, which takes place in a process they call *legitimate peripheral participation*. According to Lave and Wenger, "learners inevitably participate in communities of practitioners and . . . the mastery of knowledge and skill requires newcomers to move toward full participation in the sociocultural practices of a community" (p.29). "Rather than learning by replicating the performances of others or by acquiring knowledge transmitted in instruction, we suggest that learning occurs through centripetal participation in the learning curriculum of the ambient community" (p.100). In other words, learning occurs as the learner moves from legitimate participation at the periphery of the community of practitioners toward more and more central participation ("centripetal participation") in the most meaningful and important aspects of professional practice.

By definition, participation is characterized by two variables: legitimacy and peripherality. First, the learner must have legitimate access to the community of practice. In other words, in order to learn, the learner needs to have direct involvement in the community's productive activity. But that participation should be peripheral: the learner participates in real activities, "but only to a limited degree and with limited responsibility for the ultimate product as a whole" (Hanks, 1991, p.14). Rather than being segregated from professional practice, learners should be a part of but peripheral to that practice, gradually moving from the periphery toward the center.

The need for access, as well as the control and selection for it, are inherent in communities of practice, making access liable to manipulation. Thus, according to Lave and Wenger (1991), legitimate peripherality has an "ambivalent status: Depending on the organization of access, legitimate peripherality can either promote or prevent legitimate participation" (p.103). Legitimate participation can be prevented by the lack of carefully planned, successive experiences which more and more closely resemble the core practices of the community. The presence of such planned experiences should promote learning.

Secondary Teaching Methods as Legitimate Peripheral Participation in a Community of Practice

Clearly the community of practice for secondary preservice teachers is to be found in secondary schools rather than college campuses. Student teaching is designed, of course, to provide direct involvement in the community's productive activity. But the opportunity for centripetal participation is excessively accelerated in student teaching as a result of the constraints of college calendars and state regulations. Delaying involvement in the community's productive activity until the student teaching semester ignores the "developmental cycles of that community" (Lave and Wenger, 1991, p.100) and requires students to assume full responsibilities too quickly. At the start of traditional student teaching, the student jumps from one role to the other without the benefit of carefully planned centripetal activities. The result is what happened to our social studies student teacher.

What was needed in Linfield's program was legitimate *peripheral* participation prior to the student teaching experience. The secondary aiding experience our student completed was primarily, if not exclusively, an observational experience. And it could be argued that students were, at best, participating in the community of teacher aides rather than teachers. That is, rarely did they actually participate in other than the clerical duties of teaching. Their observations and assistance activities included only limited social engagement with teachers about the practice of teaching. Furthermore, as is common in small colleges like Linfield, the required secondary methods and management and discipline courses are necessarily general in nature given the range of majors represented. But as Shulman (1987, 1989) makes clear, expert teachers not only know how to teach in an expert fashion but they also know their subjects as experts, and they can draw connections between the subject and the methodology and make decisions based on these connections and the needs of their students. Legitimate peripheral participation would include time for secondary preservice teachers to discuss with expert teachers in their subject fields these connections between subject, method, and students using examples from classroom experiences where secondary teacher and college student were co-participants. There were no such opportunities in our prior program.

In extending Shulman's thesis, Cochran and her colleagues (Cochran, *et al.*, 1993) point out the continuous nature of learning about content teaching and re-phrase Shulman's term as Pedagogical Content *Knowing*. This constructivist view adds the dimension of the environmental context of learning to Shulman's formulation of subject matter content, pedagogy, and students, according to Cochran et al., and necessitates that teacher education take place within the appropriate environmental context. "Teachers can learn about students best by working directly with them because *live* teaching permits the direct interaction that shows ideas in use and opens the way to negotiating paths of understanding" (p. 267). In order to foster pedagogical content knowing, it seemed to us, teacher education should take place in the schools themselves.

The Climate of Change in Oregon Schools

At about the same time these conversations were occurring, the Oregon State Legislature passed into law a bill now known as Oregon's Education Act for the 21st Century. Originally called "House Bill 3565" as it worked its way through the legislative process, this act has begun to change the way schools work in this state. Although subsequent legislatures have chipped away at the reforms required by the initial law, many schools are proceeding along the lines laid out in 1991.

As important as the actual reforms mandated has been the climate established by the law. While some educators have decided to wait out what they see as yet another passing bandwagon, the expectation in most districts has been that change is coming and therefore experimentation and creative approaches are supported. For us at Linfield, this climate of change meant that our proposal was greeted as a welcome part of the broader movement to reform schools. Teachers at MHS who were most actively involved in state-wide efforts to implement the new law were among those who willingly joined us in planning this project to change the way secondary teachers are trained.

On the Linfield campus a similarly fortuitous set of circumstances was developing. Declining resources for public institutions have meant increasing applications to Linfield. Also at about this time appeared the first of a series of very positive ratings of Linfield by national publications which rank colleges and universities, in which Linfield was held up as an excellent example of a fine liberal arts institution which had contained its costs. Together these two factors helped to place the college in the enviable position of holding down growth in order to maintain the quality of a small college rather than of being forced to cut back. The college administration has always supported innovation in teaching, and this proposal received a modest stipend from the college to fund the planned adjunct salaries for high school teachers. This support has continued.

Given this positive climate, establishing an innovative secondary teacher methods block proved to be a relatively easy task. As the initial conversation between Keith and Boyd was carried to respective colleagues and administrators, the message in response was uniformly "Let's see what we can do to help this along," rather than the more typical "Here are the obstacles I can predict." Our colleagues in the Education Department were most supportive, since we were able to share the considerable literature supporting site-based teacher education programs with them (Ashton, 1992; Boyd, 1990). College administrators, as mentioned above, were also supportive and even found the discretionary funds to provide not only adjunct salaries but also additional load credits for Keith to manage the site arrangements. Teachers at MHS were enthusiastic, since they knew that Linfield attracted a high caliber of student and they had worked with our student teachers on a regular basis. And the McMinnville School District administration, including the building principal, were in agreement that this would be a positive move, particularly when informed that it would cost no additional school district monies.

The New Program

The essence of the secondary methods block innovation, simple as it sounds, was to move the eight semester credits of the block into the high school. College classes meet for a two-period chunk in a high school classroom five days a week, with some of that time split off for students to meet with cooperating teachers and work in their classrooms. In addition, the best high school teachers in each department are hired as Linfield adjunct faculty to teach the content-area methods courses (methods of teaching social studies, for example), and this group of adjuncts is part of the team which plans the semester-long methods block. Linfield faculty members cover high school classes if necessary so that MHS faculty can visit the Linfield courses down the hall as guest lecturers, and MHS faculty members coordinate their content methods discussions with the Linfield courses in general methods and management/discipline.

One of the reasons this works so well is that MHS maintains an open campus for lunch, and so every teacher has the same lunch hour. We use an open fourth-period classroom for Linfield classes and stay through the lunch hour; MHS faculty who have a fourth-hour class can join us during fifth period. Linfield students are assigned to an individual MHS teacher (who may not be the adjunct content methods teacher) and are responsible to find an additional period each day during which they can work in that classroom.

The contextual elements of holding methods classes in a high school classroom during the middle of the day cannot be over-estimated. We are subject to the same scheduling shifts, the same announcements, the same hallway noise as all other high school teachers. We have only to walk the halls on the way to class to get a feel for the life of a large modern high school. Cooperating teachers, school administrators, and counselors are just a few steps away and are happy to be resources for the Linfield students if their schedules permit. Library, computer lab, snack bar, ESL and handicapped resource rooms, and police patrols are all part of this context, unlike the ivory tower classrooms on campus. The hidden curriculum comes to life for our students, as do the varied faces of the student body. Communication with practicing educators can and does occur in many serendipitous and informal ways, adding dimensions to our students' learning which would not be remotely possible without this on-site experience. In Lave and Wenger's terms, students are engaged in *legitimate peripheral participation* in the life of the school from the start of the methods block.

Most importantly, the tightly-woven planning which links general methods courses, content methods courses, and in-classroom practicum experiences allows students to establish connections among all of these elements, to seek and make sense of patterns in high school teaching. Students read about and discuss cooperative grouping practices in the general methods courses, they find out during their meetings with their content methods instructors (MHS teachers) how these practices play out in math or music classes, for example, and then they work in a classroom which is using cooperative groups. These patterns are con-sciously planned by the Linfield-MHS team, so that students are not left to discover on their own that classroom organization depends on student characteristics coupled with curriculum linked to teaching methods and activities, for example.

Again to use Lave and Wenger's terms, the Linfield/MHS program now provides students with planned centripetal participation in the community of practice so that there is a seamless experience from the periphery to the center of practice, the role of teacher. This careful planning and communication among college and school-based professionals is what distinguishes Linfield's program from internships, for example. Full-year experiences provide the legitimate peripheral participation, but there may be no better connection between campus-based courses and the classroom realities of each placement than in Linfield's old program. Situating the methods block on site allows those connections to happen, providing the

114

contextual element necessary for a deeper understanding of teaching and learning in secondary schools, a holistic understanding of teaching which Eisner calls "educational connoisseurship" (Eisner, 1994). Leaving those important understandings to chance has been one of the failings of traditional teacher education programs. Linfield's program takes a long step toward making them real for each student.

Growing Pains and Future Directions

After four increasingly successful years of the new program, some adjustments are called for. MHS teachers who have been part of the program from the beginning need some relief. We need to expand the pool of master teachers who understand the program and are willing to work with us. Our increasing enrollment is another source of strain on the high school teaching and administrative staffs as they continue to accept our practicum and student teachers. Future plans call for expanding the number of program sites from the single high school to the two middle schools in the district as well. By recruiting master teachers at each of the middle schools and rotating among the three schools by semester, we can maintain the strengths of our current program while adding the important middle school experience for all of our secondary education students. Fortunately, official District and College support remains strong, buttressed by the overwhelmingly positive experiences of all the program participants. We expect this partnership between Linfield's secondary teacher education program and the McMinnville public schools to continue and to prosper.

References

Ashton, P. T. (Ed.). (1992). Theme: Professional development schools. *Journal of Teacher Education, 43* (1).

Ashton, P.T. (Ed.). (1992). Theme: Partners in school restructuring. *Journal of Teacher Education, 43* (4).

Boyd, P.C. (1994). Professional school reform and public school renewal: Portrait of a partnership. *Journal of Teacher Education, 45* (2), 132-139.

Eisner, E. (1994). *The Educational Imagination* (3rd ed.). New York: Macmillan.

Hanks, W. F. (1991). Forward by William F. Hanks (pp. 13-24). In J. Lave & E. Wenger, *Situated learning: Legitimate peripheral participation.* New York: Cambridge University Press.

Lave, J. & Wenger, E. (1991). *Situated learning: Legitimate peripheral participation.* New York: Cambridge University Press.

Shulman, L. (1987). Knowledge and teaching: Foundations of the new reform. *Harvard Educational Review, 57* (1), 1-22.

Shulman, L. (1989). Toward a pedagogy of substance. *AAHE Journal, 41* (10), 8-13.

Only Connect! A Collaborative Project in the Humanities

Marjorie Checkoway, Richard Sax, Ernie Nolan

Madonna University (Michigan)

Ernest Boyer described education as "a seamless web" in which "all levels of education are inextricably connected" (1994, p. 10). Madonna University has initiated two projects supported by the National Endowment for the Humanities which have attempted to foster collaboration within the university between liberal arts and education faculty—and between university faculty and K-12 teachers outside the institution. All the participants are key mentors in the preparation of teachers.

State of the Humanities in the State of Michigan

At present, humanities educators in Michigan are concerned about the educational priorities of the State. Two trends are becoming increasingly antithetical to the goals of humanities education: (1) the proliferation of "tech prep" and "school-to-work" approaches to K-12 curriculum decision-making which emphasize employability skills over reflective and speculative habits of mind; and (2) an over-emphasis on standardized test scores, particularly the Michigan Education Assessment Program (MEAP) scores which are scrutinized by the public. Classroom teachers feel increasing pressure to abandon the content and methodologies of the traditional humanities disciplines and "teach to the test" to prepare their students for the MEAP assessment. This has become such a priority for some local districts that curricula are being redesigned, and valuable class time is given over to practice and drill for the test. Teachers therefore have a crucial need to use as effectively as possible the time they can devote to ideas and culture, to be clearsighted about the goals of humanities education, to be prepared to engage students in activities that will capture their imagination and connect in relevant ways to their lives.

Shared Responsibilities

The goal of the first project initiated by Madonna University, "Integrating the Humanities and Teacher Preparation," was to promote a sense of shared responsibility for the preparation of teachers among the faculties of the traditional humanities disciplines and the faculty of the teacher preparation program. The project recognized the need for establishing a more integrated educational experience for prospective teachers, built on a common knowledge base in the humanities—including classical and multicultural texts—as a means of enriching the quality of teaching of these students as they graduate and enter Michigan's schools. The project was concerned with moving faculty members from disciplinary isolation into an interdisciplinary community engaged in conversation about multiple perspectives on the nature of learning, diverse ways of knowing, and the role and value of education in our society. The primary vehicles for achieving this goal were the shared experience of a colloquium series, six colloquia per year in which we interpreted texts and shared perspectives and a two-week summer workshop each year for two years. With a common foundation of shared values as well as of multiple perspectives, those responsible for teaching future teachers—both from liberal arts and education—have become more willing and eager to dismantle a dichotomy of liberal and career education to be replaced by a more integrated model which emphasizes connections between ideas and action.

Professors in the Schools

Madonna University developed a Professors in the Schools program as part of the initial project, "Integrating the Humanities and Teacher Education." We developed pairings whereby a Madonna professor (in English, Religious Studies & Philosophy, Japanese Studies, or History) has teamed with a K-12 teacher in a similar content area in order to make curricular connections and to share pedagogical strategies. For example, many 11th-grade English classes in Michigan focus on American literature, and many 12th-grade English classes focus on British literature, sometimes even sharing certain texts that might be taught in college-level American and British literature survey courses. In our vainglorious innocence at the beginning of the grant, we assumed that the curricular connections would be directed by the university professors (read: top-down), while pedagogical strategies would be best provided by the K-12 teachers (read: bottom-up). Of course, the actual sharing process became much more fluid and even recursive. Theories and strategies of content and pedagogy are considered and evaluated as we approach issues of content as well as our shared roles as partners in education.

The mandated requirements of the professors in the Schools program were relatively few: on-site visits by both participants at both the K-12 school and on the Madonna campus; telephone, E-mail, fax, and/or personal discussions; a written end document, either a simple evaluation of the team experience or, in some cases, a teaching module created for either the given K-12 level or the college classroom. It was important for us to emphasize, however, that the focus was more philosophical than ad hoc: we were providing lifelong strategies for professional development, not lecture notes for next Tuesday's class—though, of course, the expectation was that there would indeed be applicability in the very near future to the classroom. Our philosophical focus included such questions as: What does it mean to be a teacher in a democratic society? What sort of education should we attempt to provide? How do we accomplish our goals? How might we change what we do to serve better our various constituencies? (Please see Appendix for a complete list of prompting questions for Professors in the Schools participants.)

Yet, the pairings had tangible outcomes as well. One especially fruitful pairing involved a Madonna English professor with a high school humanities teacher. Each educator not only visited the other's classes but actually taught specific sessions at the other campus on certain class days, and a level of sharing of both content and pedagogy developed which continues today. The Madonna professor continues to draw on this experience in her current role as NEH Distinguished Professor in the Humanities for 1995-97. The high school humanities teacher was acknowledged for her efforts at a school board meeting when her participation in the project activities and her influence in curriuclum development were noted.

The Goal: K-16 Education

The second project that Madonna University initiated, "Bridging the Gap Between Knowing and Teaching in the Humanities: A Collaborative Project," is ongoing and builds on the success of the first initiative.

While we strengthened collaboration within the institution's boundaries with the first project and began to make connections with K-12 classrooms and educators, we knew we had to leap more aggressively across the boundary which is more difficult to span. As we thought about

118

providing future teachers with a stronger grounding in the humanities, we considered how we could build bridges across the parallel streams which inform professional practice: the higher education classroom and the field experiences in the K-12 classroom. Surely, these two worlds of education should be communicating with one another in order to foster a K-16 continuum of education.

Therefore, in keeping with our commitment to span the university-school chasm, the current project provides professional development opportunities to a selected group of K-12 teachers and administrators, utilizing the expertise of humanities and education faculty members. The project promotes active pedagogy in the humanities by providing resources to strengthen and enrich the teaching of in-service teachers.

Through a colloquium series and summer workshops, teachers and administrators focus on humanities texts with scholars who serve as facilitators. In addition, Humanities Resource Teams, composed of both K-12 and University educators, meet regularly to carry the impetus of the project back to the school districts by formulating strategies and developing mechanisms to promote humanities education. The teams, through meetings, discussions, and classroom visitations, address the practical dimensions of strengthening both curriculum and pedagogy in the schools. This activity opens the channels of communication between primary players in educational reform—in the University and in the local schools—who often do not have access to each other and therefore cannot engage in substantive discourse. These teams have taken the efforts of the Professors in the Schools one step further by involving department chairs and administrators who are in positions to influence program policy and changes.

Instead of the two-person collaboration, the new teams will involve four educators: one MU humanities professor; one MU education professor; one K-12 teacher; one K-12 administrator from the same building. The inclusion of the last member will hopefully address one of the discouraging features of earlier collaborative efforts: when the K-12 teacher and the college professor begin to change and adapt content and pedagogy, the college professor generally has free reign, aka "academic freedom" to make the change, while the K-12 teacher is often limited by the dictates of a department chair, curriculum committee, or building principal. We trust that the inclusion of an administrator at all levels of discussion in this project will allow greater and more fruitful change to occur.

A final professional development opportunity is a series of workshops offered by the University for pre-service and in-service teachers entitled, "Approaches to Teaching . . .," which focus on commonly taught texts in K-12 language arts, English, history, and humanities classes.

Reflection and Reconsideration

As we have discussed texts and come together across the disciplinary boundaries, we have considered and reflected on both content and pedagogy in humanities instruction. Faculty members have had the opportunity to enrich their perspectives across cultures through literature and non-fiction as well as to discuss pedagogical implications for K-12 classrooms. Our readings have reflected the diversity of cultures of our society and have emphasized our priorities to tap into the richness of multiple cultural perspectives.

We think we have become a community of learners. We have collaborated to provide the future teachers, which both education and liberal arts faculty have in common with, a stronger grounding in the humanities, emphasizing the diverse cultures which constitute our human community and which mirror the cultural backgrounds of our students in Southeastern Michigan. For example, the 1995 Summer Workshop, with Madonna University faculty and K-12 teachers as participants, focused on connecting cultures and crossing borders and boundaries through studying African, Islamic, and Japanese literature. The Detroit area has a large African-American population, the highest concentration of people from the Middle East outside of the Middle East, and a growing population of Japanese students because of the auto industry.

One Thing Needful: The Paradigm Shift

One outcome of this project has been a paradigm shift, one which recognizes that we teach within a broad community, not just within the shell of our institutions and departments. The old and existing paradigm could perhaps best be articulated by Andre Gide's paraphrase of a comment supposedly made by the French painter Edgar Degas, "Art criticism! What an absurdity! . . . the Muses never talk among themselves; each one works in her own domain; and when they aren't working, they dance" (1967, p. 137). This passage can be used as a metaphor for how many of us in the humanities used to consider the mentorship of our majors in teacher education: it wasn't our responsibility, our bailiwick, our demesne (yes, in the medieval fiefdom sense of the word!). Each of us was considered to be a free and independent Muse who should not be sullied with such ad hoc social science work as guiding the development of pre-service and student teachers.

The experiences of the collaborative project have helped to create a paradigm shift, and our attitudes have changed. In the words of E.M. Forster in *Howard's End*, the new watchword quotation has become: "Only connect!" (1921, p. 186). We must connect in a number of ways: humanities faculty members with education faculty members; college professors with K-12 teachers; pre-service and student teachers with current teachers at all levels. The responsibility, for example, of "content" student teacher visitations, which used to devolve to the English Department Chair by default, is now shared by most of the full-time faculty members in English because of the relatively new realization that if —in the words of an African proverb—it takes an entire village to educate its youth, then the entire department should share both the burden and the opportunity (which combine to form the responsibility) to direct its neophyte teachers.

Recommendations

We have deduced a number of conclusions from these experiences. It is clear that a college professor can be given released time to participate in such a project; for elementary and secondary school teachers, however, it becomes problematic to drop a class or to get a frequent substitute, even if the school district is willing to provide such support. Both remuneration and institutional support must be provided to the K-12 teacher. Especially with budget cuts affecting virtually every school district in the state of Michigan, professional development is being cut altogether or significantly reduced at the district and at the school level. We have been successful in recruiting K-12 teachers to our Professors in the Schools program through emphasizing that what we are offering is professional development at no actual financial cost to the schools.

Rationale for Selection of K-12 Participants

In terms of strategies for selection of K-12 teachers, we have learned not necessarily to go through the administrative channels of a Curriculum Director, Assistant Superintendent, or Principal. These persons do not always know the best, or most willing, teachers in their systems or buildings. We wanted to follow protocol, and we did, though this did not always provide a teacher ready to engage in such a project. Instead, we have learned to contact teachers we have met, seen, visited, heard about—we pitch the project to them, and if they agree, at that point, we get the necessary administrative clearance to create the collaborative agreement. As is the case in writing and composition theory, the process at times is as important as the ultimate product: the process of interchange is worthwhile and vital to all parties concerned, and one need not be overly outcomes-based about such partnerships, at least in the initial stages.

What has already occurred, however, is a clear paradigm shift among our humanities professor colleagues. We have learned that we are all education professors, especially those of us who are humanities professors. We need to be more explicit not only about what we teach but also about how we teach and why it is important to teach it. We have learned that we teach not only on campus (whether it be a college or university campus or a high school, middle school, or elementary school building) but also in the region (SE Michigan), the state of Michigan, the USA, the planet Earth. We are preparing students for life as citizens in what Marshall McLuhan so accurately termed a "global village," and we need to educate our students so that they may become productive citizens in that community. We have learned that we can no longer afford to pass the buck, to blame the next level down: college professors blaming high school teachers who blame middle school teachers who blame elementary school teachers who blame pre-school teachers, and they all chorus together to blame parents and the surrounding the community! Instead, we need to communicate, to take responsibility, to realize that we are all partners in education. We can no longer teach in splendid isolation!

As our learning community has broadened, teacher education students have experienced changes in their classrooms: both in the university classroom and in the field placement classroom. Humanities professors are now focusing more on pedagogical implications related to content. They are involving a broader variety of teaching strategies and suggesting ways of relating material to younger learners. Education faculty are including more literature-based materials in their courses, not only promoting interdisciplinary learning but modeling it. Furthermore, the collaborative relations between the University and K-12 educators have enabled the field-placement mentors to know the University program better, to broaden their perspectives about knowing and learning and multicultural literature, all being major focus issues of the project, and to develop a more literature-based curriculum as well.

Preservice teachers are the beneficiaries of these initiatives. They are the partners in the collaboration who experience life in the classrooms of the project participants. The enrichment of their respective mentors is translating to more purposeful attention to the value of the humanities in the classroom, to diverse pedagogical strategies, and to the modeling of the value of collaboration itself. A stimulated teacher, operating within a new paradigm of shared responsibility for future teachers, is a teacher who can lead others toward a wide vision of the spectrum of knowing and learning.

Conclusion

In order to continue and build on these initiatives, we need to foster the concept of K-16 education on a regional basis. Especially considering the fact that we teach at a university that is comprised principally of students from local communities, it behooves us to dissolve the artificial, as well as the physical, structures that divide a university from the K-12 schools that send it students—and to which the university will send back prepared teachers. With distance learning and satellite campus locations, we no longer teach only in our home classrooms, anyway. We need to take the next step to assure that we are truly becoming, with K-12 teachers and educators, partners in education.

References

Boyer, E. (1994). *New directions for collaboration. On common ground, (2)*, 10-11.

Gide, A. (1967). *Journals, 1889-1949.* (J. O'Brien, Trans.) Harmondsworth: Penguin.

Forster, E.M. (1921). *Howards end*. New York: Knopf.

Appendix A

N.B. These questions are meant to be suggestive and speculative, not definitive. The individual pairs of teacher-professors should redefine their own sort and level of cooperation, as long as it is consistent with the overall goals of the grant. We do not expect that any single pair of educators will address all of these questions, but we hope that the eight pairs of educators over the next two years will address all of these issues.

Questions for Professors in the Schools Participants to Consider:

- Have humanities faculty members become familiar with the pedagogical demands of K-12 teaching?

- Have humanities faculty members had the opportunity to share their own content expertise with teachers and students, K-12?

- In what manner have the teaching skills of the team members been enhanced through this exchange of expertise?

- Do you feel that it is appropriate/possible for the Madonna University professor and the K-12 teacher to co-author and implement humanities units appropriate to their level?

- To what degree have team members become better prepared to strengthen the humanities curriculum, both in the K-12 setting as well as in the Madonna University teacher preparation program?

- Has this cooperative venture allowed you to consider new teaching-learning strategies geared to the cognitive development and skills of students?

- Has this cooperative experience provided insights and ideas which the Madonna University professor can incorporate into his/her contact with future teachers?

Maryville College & Secondary Educators: Linking Theory with Practice

Terry L. Simpson
Marcia J. Keith

Maryville College (Tennessee)

Introduction

The current educational reform movement has been focused in part on defining a new relationship between K-12 teachers and college faculty. Some examples are: (1) using classroom teachers as mentors for preservice and new teachers (Timar & Kirp, 1989; Kennedy, 1991; Meade, 1991); (2) involving local school districts in teacher education (Roth, 1989; Meade, 1991); and developing processes that support collaboration between college faculty and classroom teachers in the training of new teachers (Orlich, 1989; Roth, 1989; Timar, 1989; Irvin, 1990; Kagan, 1991; Meade, 1991; Kennedy, 1991). Irvin (1990), for instance, has advocated the formation of a new faculty entity, "a teacher training faculty," a faculty of public school and higher education personnel. This "teacher training faculty" would be jointly responsible for the professional development of preservice teachers. In spite of this message from reformers in teacher education, higher education has rarely engaged in truly collaborative programs for preparing new teachers (Grossman & Brantigan, 1992). Our paper will describe an effective collaborative program that links the Maryville College education faculty with public school secondary teachers (field adjuncts) and Maryville College faculty from the academic disciplines. The thrust of our program is not only consistent with the reformers' recommendations, but more importantly, it is consistent with the philosophy of the Maryville College Division of Education.

125

Maryville College Rationale

We view teaching as a minded performance, that is, as a purposeful intellectual activity carried out within a particular context. Our goal is to provide our graduates with those understandings (skills, abilities, knowledge, and beliefs) that are directly related to the wise execution of the tasks of teaching. Figure 1 (Reynolds, 1992) represents the

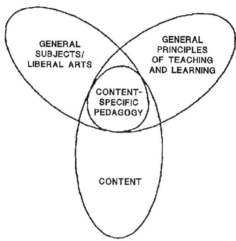

FIGURE 1. *Domains of Understanding* [In Reynolds, A. (1992). What is competent beginning teaching? A review of the literature. *Review of Educational Research, 62*(1), 1-36.]

relevant domains of these "understandings." It can be seen that content-specific pedagogy (understandings related to appropriate teaching strategies, methods and representations of the subject matter, and understandings related to the students being taught) integrates aspects from all other domains. Even so, such understandings are not sufficient to prepare successful teachers. In addition, conceptual knowledge must be linked with procedural knowledge for the minded performance that we view as teaching to occur. It is not surprising that one of the major complaints about teacher education is that it is too theoretical and not relevant to the real world of teaching. In our view, this statement indicates that the linkage has not been carefully forged. We believe that direct contact between our students and qualified secondary teachers will help ameliorate the conditions which give rise to this complaint. Figure 2 represents our interpretation of how this linkage may be encouraged. Licensure students observe and reflect upon effective instructional models demonstrated both at Maryville College by College faculty and in the secondary classrooms of Field Adjuncts. In addition,

Conceptual Understanding — Viewing Models — Safe Practice — Procedural Knowledge			
(From the Domains)	- Classes - Explorations - Videos - Practicum	- Mico-teach Peers Small Groups Whole Class - Full Class Period Practicum - Student Teaching	- Contextual - Explicit - Specific

FIGURE 2. Encouraging the Linkage

they participate in safe micro-teaching experiences both at the College and in secondary classrooms during the Practicum. Further, Field Adjuncts evaluate their practicum students' written reflections on the micro-teaching experiences. These experiences help bridge the gap which exists between conceptual understanding and procedural knowledge. As a result, the direct relationship between what we know about (theory) and what we know how to do (practice) is made explicit as Field Adjuncts model effective teaching practices in their classrooms, reflect on that practice and provide our students with classroom "safe" teaching opportunities. Field Adjuncts have become essential team members as the College strives to develop well prepared first-year teachers.

Development of the Practicum

In 1992 a summer workshop funded by an Annenberg Grant was held to develop a course for secondary licensure students. Twelve secondary teachers from five separate school districts in eastern Tennessee, ranging from suburban to rural, met for a week in a retreat setting on the campus of Maryville College. These secondary teachers represented the disciplines in which the College offers secondary licensure. For two days they met with Maryville College professors from the same academic disciplines and discussed current issues related to teaching and learning. By the end of the week these secondary teachers had developed curriculum guides for a content specific course in pedagogy in each of the disciplines. These guides listed goals and objectives for the course as well as suggested activities from which individual course syllabi could be developed. This workshop and the subsequent curriculum guides have provided cohesion to the Practicum while permitting the flexibility needed for the integrity of the disciplines' content specific pedagogy.

Recruitment of Field Adjunct Faculty

After the curriculum guides had been developed, the next step was to recruit qualified secondary teachers, who together with an education professor from the College were to function as a "Field Adjunct Faculty" in order to team teach the sections of the Practicum. A number of public school administrators as well as Maryville College administrators were consulted concerning the criteria for selecting the teachers. Finally, the following criteria were identified to be used in the selection process:

1. An appropriate graduate degree;

2. Three years teaching experience in their discipline;

3. Letter of recommendation from their immediate supervisor;

4. Letter of recommendation from a colleague in the same discipline;

5. Evidence that they were active in a professional organization related to their discipline.

After the criteria were identified, the College began to advertise the positions in area school districts. In addition, a member of the Education Division of the College visited faculty chairpersons at a local high school. As a result, well-qualified secondary teachers have been appointed to each of the content specific Practica. These secondary teachers are classified as field adjunct faculty of the College, are paid by the College, and are awarded privileges of being a Maryville College faculty member (such as library use and passes to athletic events). The field adjunct faculty are regularly involved with other faculty members from the College in discussions concerning issues related to teacher education.

Teaching the Practicum

Secondary licensure students enroll in the Practicum during the semester prior to student teaching; however, a number of conditions must be met prior to this semester. First, the student must have completed Level I Screening. When a student completes this screening process, the student is permitted to take professional development courses. Second, the student must successfully complete Education 301, Models of Classroom Management and Instruction. Only then is the licensure student assigned to the field adjunct in the student's area of licensure.

As soon as the students have been assigned to the Practicum for a new semester, each field adjunct faculty member develops a syllabus based on the curriculum guide. During the first class meeting, a Maryville College education professor, all field adjunct faculty and the licensure students meet for orientation and an overview of the course. For the first month of the course, the students begin research into current issues facing their respective disciplines under the guidance of the "teacher training faculty," that is, a member of the Maryville College education faculty and the appropriate field adjunct. During the fifth week of the semester the licensure students begin working directly with the field adjuncts in high school classrooms.

Student assignments and activities vary according to the nature of the discipline; however, a consistency in the requirements has been achieved. First, the students complete their research papers or a series of brief research projects on a current issue facing their respective disciplines. Such an assignment might include investigating the cause of math anxiety among girls in secondary math classes or evaluating the changes brought about by a multicultural emphasis in American literature classes. The Field Adjuncts and Maryville College education faculty, in light of their own professional experiences, guide the students in selecting appropriate topics.

Second, the students develop lesson plans and teach classes with "real" students under the close supervision of the Field Adjuncts. They teach advanced, grade level and below grade level students and then discuss the different strategies with their teachers. In biology, for example, the licensure students plan and teach both lab and non-lab classes. The lab classes enable the licensure students to deal with lab safety and chemical security in a "real world" setting. These experiences enable our licensure students to preclude many problems normally faced for the first time during student teaching.

Third, the Field Adjuncts model effective teaching practices with real high school students. For example, the group may discuss effective questioning techniques during a discussion session, and as a result, the Field Adjunct models these techniques the next morning in class.

Fourth, the licensure students meet once a week with their assigned Field Adjuncts to discuss their research, the assigned readings, their lesson plans, or perhaps effective teaching practices. Whether the meeting takes place at 7:00 a.m. before school starts or in the evening at the teacher's home, time is found to meet as a group. At this point, the Field Adjunct becomes a mentor in the truest sense. Often the relationship continues long after our licensure students get teaching positions.

By working closely with selected classroom teachers, secondary licensure students see a clear relationship between research-based theory and their practice as effective classroom teachers. Content specific pedagogy has become more than an abstract term in the Maryville College Teacher Education Program.

Role of the Liberal Arts Faculty

In many colleges and universities the teacher licensure students are often transferred (during the junior or senior year) to the department of education never again to have contact with the professors in their academic departments. This is not the case at Maryville College. A professor from each academic department in which the College offers teacher licensure has been trained by the Education Division to assist in the supervision of student teachers. These professors must recommend licensure students for student teaching and then supervise the student teachers in the critical area of competency in the content of the teaching field. Therefore, all secondary licensure students are supervised by the public school cooperating teachers and Maryville College professors both from the education and academic departments. At the conclusion of student teaching, these professors from the academic departments must recommend the students for licensure. As a result of this collaboration among the departments and divisions at the College, teacher education has not been isolated from the main academic focus of the College.

Evaluation

During the 1994 Fall Semester the licensure students taking the practicum completed an evaluation of the course using an instrument developed by the Maryville College faculty for use in the evaluation of all courses and professors. In Table 1 we have identified the items that are applicable to the Practicum. The lowest rating given by the licensure students on any item pertaining to the competency of the instructor

---

Evaluation of the Practicum
By Maryville College Licensure Students
Numerical Scale: Low 1 to 5 High

Item	Average Rating
1. The instructor showed enthusiasm for the subject of the course.	4.6
2. The instructor exhibited sound knowledge of the subject matter.	5.0
3. The instructor established a stimulating environment which challenged me to think and participate actively.	4.4
4. The instructor created an atmosphere of respect for my ideas, opinions and questions.	4.8
5. The required readings contributed to my learning.	4.5
6. Assignments contributed to my understanding of the course content.	5.0
7. The course challenged me to think seriously about and to become involved in the subject.	4.4

Table 1

---

or the effectiveness of the course was 4.4 on a numerical scale of 1 to 5. On the items addressing the expertise of the secondary teachers who serve as Field Adjunct Faculty and the relevance of the assignments in the Practicum, the licensure students rated both items a perfect 5.0.

In the process of evaluating a course, the written comments of students often give added insight, especially when the evaluation data are generated from a small number of students. Below are examples of comments that we have received from our licensure students.

- This teacher is very dedicated and enjoys teaching.

- This was a wonderful experience. There is nothing like learning from the best in the field. I feel extremely fortunate to have worked with such a professional and well-known teacher. The first hand knowledge given directly to me was, and will be invaluable.

- It was wonderful to get first hand experience.

- Good preparation for student teaching.

- Very energetic and enthusiastic.

- He makes me want to be in the classroom.

In addition to a course evaluation of the Practicum, licensure students complete a self-evaluation of their perceived competence in professional knowledge and skill outcomes. This self evaluation is completed at the conclusion of student teaching. Table 2 lists the knowledge and skill outcomes assigned specifically to the Practicum. Our graduates report that they are very confident in the knowledge and skill outcomes assigned to the Practicum with the exception of Item Five. Consequently, exposing our licensure students to the appropriate professional journals and organizations in the specific teaching fields has become a priority both in the Student Teaching Seminar as well as in the Practicum.

Besides the program evaluations that are administered on campus, the College participates in the Tennessee Teacher Education Follow-up Survey. Data from this survey are tabulated by the Center for Research in Educational Policy at Memphis State University (see Table 3). We have identified two items in this survey that address the issue of efficacy as it applies to beginning teachers. When the Practicum was being developed, we theorized that the mentoring of secondary licensure students by field adjuncts would help to develop a sense of efficacy in our graduates. Table 3 compares responses from our graduates of the final year of the old program prior to the implementation of the Practicum to our graduates during the first two years of the Practicum on

Self Evaluation:
Maryville College Secondary Licensure Students

Knowledge and Skill Outcomes Assigned to the Practicum	Self Rating		
	Very Confident	Confident	Weak
1. Ability to integrate resources effectively such as community resources, resource persons, audio/visual materials, and computers.	89%	6%	5%
2. Ability to identify long range instructional goals and to sequence related short range instructional objectives appropriate for developmental level and subject area.	83%	17%	0
3. Ability to select, justify, and implement curricular content and instructional strategies appropriate to students' needs; ability to plan for instruction including the development of units and daily lessons; ability to use a variety of research-based instructional strategies.	83%	11%	6%
4. Ability to relate learning to real life experiences of the students.	94%	0	6%
5. Ability to converse about appropriate journals and professional organizations in education and in the teaching field(s).		6%	22%

Table 2

Tennessee Teacher Education Follow-up Survey

I. Succeed as a Beginning Teacher

Last Class of Secondary Licensure Students Before the Practicum		Secondary Licensure Students Who Have Taken the Practicum	
Weak - Adequate	22.7%	Weak - Adequate	12.5%
Strong - Very Strong	72.8%	Strong - Very Strong	83.3%

II. Make a Difference with Students

Last Class of Secondary Licensure Students Before the Practicum		Secondary Licensure Students Who Have Taken the Practicum	
Weak - Adequate	22.7%	Weak - Adequate	12.5%
Strong - Very Strong	72.7%	Strong - Very Strong	83.3%

Table 3

the two items that address teacher efficacy. While the increase has not been dramatic, the data indicate a slight increase in a positive direction.

After careful analyses of the evaluation data from our licensure students, we have concluded that our students have the highest regard for the enthusiasm and expertise of the secondary teachers who serve as Field Adjunct Faculty. Furthermore, they consider the Practicum as one of the most beneficial aspects of their professional development.

In addition to licensure students evaluating the Practicum, we have asked the Field Adjunct Faculty to evaluate the impact of the Practicum on the professional development of our students. They were asked to respond to the following question: "In what ways does the Practicum strengthen the professional development of Maryville College licensure students?" Examples of their responses are listed below.

- Very individualized, practical field experience.

- It effectively lengthens the field experience to two semesters.

- Stresses the importance of interaction with colleagues in the teaching field.

- Provides good supervision and mentoring.

- Provides opportunities to see different teaching and learning styles before student teaching.

- Gives students a "real link" with a colleague in the public schools.

- Exposes students to the secondary school environment before student teaching.

The consistency in the evaluations of the Practicum both by licensure students and the Field Adjunct Faculty enables us to conclude that our program is effective, and it bridges the gap between theory and practice.

Not only is the Practicum beneficial to our licensure students, but it is also a source of professional renewal to those secondary teachers who serve as Field Adjunct Faculty. Shortly after the program began, we were approached by an instructional supervisor who wanted to express her gratitude for the revitalizing impact that being apart of this experience had apparently had on one of her teachers. As a result of this conversation, we asked the Field Adjunct Faculty to list the personal/professional benefits that they had received by serving as a field adjunct faculty member. Examples of their responses are listed below.

- Renews my enthusiasm as I work with enthusiastic and idealistic young teachers.

- The interaction with the licensure students is refreshing.

- Professionally, it requires/enables one to keep up to date with current trends, much like a continuing education program for the teacher.

- Causes me to rethink many of my methods.

- I've had to reorganize my philosophy and thoughts about teaching.

We have discovered that effective classroom teachers have a tremendous amount of expertise to offer to licensure students. When these classroom teachers are challenged to become an essential part of a teacher training program, this result is professional renewal.

Conclusion

We believe that our collaborative program effectively links teacher education faculty with public school secondary teachers and college faculty from the academic disciplines. The typical college classroom "methods" course provides neither the field-based aspect of our program, the mentoring provided by the field adjuncts, nor the flexibility to deal with small numbers of students. Other small liberal arts institutions might well desire to implement the Maryville College collaborative model.

References

Grossman, P. L. & Brantigan, N. S. (1992). The teacher as teacher educator: New roles in professional development schools. *Kappa Delta Pi Record, 28,* 116-121.

Irvin, G. (1990). Collaborative teacher education. *Phi Delta Kappan, 71,* 622-644.

Kagan, D. M. (1991). Builders of wooden boats and the reform of teacher education: A parable. *Phi Delta Kappan, 71,* 675-677.

Kennedy, M. M. (1991). Policy issues in teacher education. *Phi Delta Kappan, 72,* 659-665.

Meade, E.J. (1991). Reshaping the clinical phase of teacher preparation. *Phi Delta Kappan, 72,* 666-669.

Orlich, D. C. (1989). Education reforms: Mistakes, misconceptions, miscues. *Phi Delta Kappan, 70,* 512-517.

Reynolds, A. (1992). What is competent beginning teaching? A review of the literature. *Review of Educational Research, 62*(1), 1-36.

Roth, R.A. (1989). The teacher education program: An endangered species. *Phi Delta Kappan, 71,* 319-323.

Timar, T. B. (1989). The politics of school restructuring. *Phi Delta Kappan, 71,* 265-277.

Timar, T. B. & Kirp, D. L. (1989). Education reform in the 1980s: Lessons from the states. *Phi Delta Kappan, 70,* 504-511.

Who Are our Partners? Reconceptualizing Teaching and Stewardship

Kathe Rasch
Mary Ellen Finch

Maryville University (Missouri)

What are the reasons for partnerships?

How does one begin a common conversation about teaching when every teacher education student comes assured that their experience tells them what teachers do every day? What happens when the very conversation about to begin is designed to create dissonance about those comfortably held beliefs? How do professional partnerships with the schools and the community provide frameworks and extended opportunities for expanding teacher education students' beliefs about their chosen profession? The program described herein chronicles some of the complex relationships and programmatic successes that have evolved at Maryville University as it prepares teachers from a very specific point of view, with particular emphasis on an initial block of three courses that serve as the introduction to teacher education at Maryville.

The attempt to describe partners and partnerships are multiple and at many levels. This is intentional. Partnerships with schools are but one way in which the professional conversation among colleagues and a shared sense of purpose are part of the Maryville Teacher Education program. The partnerships described herein involve the students, the schools, the community, and the practicing teachers at the schools and in the universities. These partnerships place the teacher in the school and the school in the community in a way that refines our teacher education students' beliefs about their roles, responsibilities, and decisions.

For the last 11 years, the authors and eight other full-time faculty have worked from a conceptual model of developing teachers who are "reflective practitioners" (Finch, 1995; Rasch, 1990). Relying heavily on a constructivist model of teaching (Fosnot, 1989; Duckworth, 1987), Maryville's model identifies four strands in which to organize that reflection. These strands are made explicit to students throughout the preservice and graduate programs. They are called:
a. School and Society
b. Curriculum and Instruction
c. Inquiry and Research
d. Development

Within the preservice program, students are placed carefully and systematically in field settings each semester. These placements and experiences are tied carefully to concurrent coursework. Partner schools have been identified by studying the school's own philosophy, the consistency of this model with Maryville's model and national curricular and instructional trends, and the school faculty's willingness to assume the additional responsibilities of teacher education. Ongoing collaborative conversations and dialogue about specific students helped school based and university based faculty to assist individual students at various stages of the program. Relationships of trust and ongoing dialogue have developed among the partners. This has set the stage for some more innovative and demanding dialogue about the nature of our work together. The joint responsibilities of all partners in the teacher education process have now begun to broaden the scope of dialogue. The program would simply not exist without the partnerships that sustain a collective professional commitment to the preparation of our teachers. At this point, attention to a wide variety of partnerships has made this commitment an impetus for a much broader voice in program development and implementation for our teacher education students.

The nature of this coursework has been changed and the dialogue about our teacher education program has reached a new level of intensity because of Maryville University's application and self study to become a member of the National Network for Educational Renewal in collaboration with Harris-Stowe State College and our partner schools for the St. Louis Public Schools and Parkway School District. New questions emerged as we began to consider our own beliefs about the moral dimensions of teaching discussed by Goodlad and his colleagues. The very process of studying our programs in relationship to the 19 postulates proposed in *Teachers for our Nation's Schools* (Goodlad, 1993) helped us to refine our relationships with all of the stakeholders in the teacher education process.

Framing much of the NNER's work (and our own work as a result) are the following questions asked often by Roger Soder:

a. What does it mean to be a liberally educated person who lives in a democracy?

And, is it different to ask,

b. What does it mean to be a liberally educated person, who is a teacher, in a democracy?

These questions helped us to redefine the nature of the partnerships necessary to develop a broad conception of teaching within a democracy for all of our teacher education candidates. They have helped us specifically expand the focus of the partnerships to include the communities surrounding the university and the schools in which the students work.

Placing the partnership in context

At Maryville, the introduction to the preservice program for all students begins operationally as students sign up for Educ 200 Field Experience in Teaching, Educ 201 School and Society, and Educ 309 Developmental Psychology I. In reality, the time frame for these classes is transformed into a carefully structured and intertwined set of experiences that involve partnerships with five schools, about 26 urban and suburban communities, and several social service agencies in those communities that provide support for school children.

Students are scheduled five mornings a week from 8 a.m. to noon. This permits the time to be structured into several phases during which different experiences provide a framework for reflection and action on all four strands, with particular emphasis on the School and Society and Research and Inquiry strands. Feiman-Nemser and Melnick (1992) and their colleagues report on their own efforts to provide such experiences reflecting on the complexity by asking:

> How should we introduce undergraduates to the study and practice of teaching . . . the course aims to loosen the grip of unexamined beliefs about teaching that students have built up through years of teacher watching and growing up in the general culture. In pursuing this aim and the intellectual habits that support it, the course exemplifies the values of liberal/professional education (p.1)

It has been essential that each of the partnerships defined by the program inform the students' reflection about what it means to teach and learn. In dialogue with the partners, we are seeking to assure that our students intentionally think about issues of equity, access, stewardship and pedagogy. Goodlad (1994) indicates that few teachers, let alone

137

teacher educators, are well grounded in thinking about the moral aspects of their work, nor do the systems in which they work support such thinking.

> The circumstances of schools and of those who work in them today are such that there must be no fuzziness in the commitment of colleges and universities involved in educating teachers. The critical importance of good teachers to good schools is such that there is no place for institutional waffling. . . .The proper commitment is essentially a moral one. (p. 43)

Our partners have helped us so that our teacher education students will be faced with dilemmas, experiences, and thinking that will help them reconceptualize their beliefs about teaching and schools.

Partnerships that consider moral stewardship

The new focus made us first re-examine the way in which students must establish partnerships with each other as colleagues. We have designed a three-week group building experience. As a cadre of 50 students coming from largely individualistic, teacher directed learning experiences, we have found it essential for the first partnership to be that of joining with each other so that they learn to rely on each other for learning, teaching, and support. A series of group building experiences include introductory activities, discussions, analysis of case studies, and activities designed to put each student in a position to delineate, discuss, and defend his/her own beliefs about dilemmas in teaching. Partnerships with each other are formed as the students are grouped by types of schooling, birth order, communities in which they grew up, and beliefs about education. A continuous regrouping of students and questioning to defend and explain beliefs begins to help them examine the questions:

What is the role of the teacher?

What are the roles of schools in your community?

What do you do if your beliefs are different than those of your colleagues?

How do you analyze and defend your beliefs about what you see and think?

How were you successful in school?

Why were you successful in school?

What are the purposes of schooling?

During this time, a second partnership with each other provides additional common, yet dissonant experience for the students. Rather than simply focusing on a soon-to-come field experience in schools where the classroom is the primary focus of analysis and learning, we believe that this partnership with the broader community is essential. In the largely racially and economically polarized St. Louis community, our own teacher education student body is mostly white, middle class, and from suburban and rural communities around St. Louis. Their aspirations to teach reveal that they see themselves teaching in a similar community because that is the way that "schools and communities are supposed to be."

Within the first four weeks, students are required to work with four of their teacher education partners to explore four very geographically-disparate schools and communities. They are grouped so that they go with people who live in different communities and they visit urban and suburban communities which, it is likely, they have never visited before. They must question anyone EXCEPT those in the schools about the schools and the communities. They are queried back in class about their experiences and speak with wonderment about similarities and differences they have observed and have many questions about how schools and communities do or do not work as partners for the education of the community's children.

This exercise sets the stage for working with school partners in yet another way. Most students have had experience (personal or vicarious through narratives from other students) with St. Louis and St. Louis County's voluntary interdistrict desegregation plan that uses cross district bussing to transport African-American students from St. Louis to many St. Louis County districts and also provides for transportation and funds for Caucasian St. Louis County students and all city students who attend St. Louis city magnet schools. Most of the teacher education students in Maryville's programs are unfamiliar with the communities in which these children live. This initial travel sets the backdrop for two other partnerships later in the semester that further emphasize the importance of the entire community in the education of all youth in the metropolitan area.

The partners in field experiences

As students begin to understand each other as partners, the classroom teachers in five partner schools prepare for the arrival of our teacher education students at their schools for their first partnership experience in schools. As mentioned earlier, partner schools in the past were identified by their own practice and its compatibility in the program. Increasingly, these partner schools have come to Maryville asking to be part of a simultaneous commitment to renewal after having heard of Maryville's work in the St. Louis Consortium for Educational Renewal.

While teacher education students spend five weeks in these schools, they often are not aware of all of the work that the teachers have done in preparation for the experience. As recently as five years ago, the teachers met with School of Education faculty that discussed the purposes for the field experiences and asked teachers to provide an opportunity for the preservice students to work in their classrooms aiding with children. Teachers provided a wealth of time and information, but the focus in relation to Maryville's program model differed greatly depending upon the teacher.

Through ongoing relationship building and the work of each school, there are now much more cohesive and formal linkages between school based and university faculty that inform their work with the Maryville students. Teachers and university faculty meet regularly to discuss and plan program rather than just discuss individual student performance. University faculty expect input from the school-based faculty regarding timing of the experience, expectations and awareness of what is being discussed in the on campus seminars that accompany the school based experiences. University faculty are participating in staff development and renewal planning at the school sites in addition to regular supervision. A Preservice Program Council has become a forum for sharing school based issues as well as teacher education program issues.

In summary, the relationship can really now be described as a "true partnership." A very specific commitment has been made in the past year to make sure that all teachers in the schools are making a conscious effort to help the teacher education students question and understand the school's efforts to face the challenges of very diverse and needful student bodies. In particular, schools have committed to helping teacher education students understand how race, class, gender, and culture are discussed with children and by the faculty as a whole. These kinds of commitment provide a forum for common conversation that may or may not have been experienced by any of the stakeholders before this time. Contact with the school children and common conversation about the children and their schools are experienced by the teacher education students and the school based and university based faculty. The systematic conversation goes a long way to make this a conversation about the broader "we" rather than one conversation in the school and another at the university. The foci for these conversations are reinforced with constant questions about the roles of teachers and the moral aspects of their work. Questioning focuses specifically on all four moral dimensions identified by Goodlad (1994, p.166). There are specific discussions about:

1. Enculturating the young in a social and political democracy;
2. Ensuring responsible stewardship of the schools;

3. Providing access to knowledge for all children and youths;
4. Practicing pedagogical nurturing.

The specific focus of these dimensions has strengthened, deepened, and focused the commitment and nature of the school/university partnerships.

A revisit to the community partners

If all goes well, the teacher education students come away from that five-week placement with more questions about the school and the community than they might have ever dreamed possible. The next examination of partnership comes from a mini-research project in which students examine (either singly or with a partner) an issue of gender, race, culture, or class that is of interest to them as a result of their experiences. In order to gain broader perspectives on the issues, they must use already introduced issue investigation strategies to formulate new insights and share the information with their class partners.

Again, information must come from many partners. Students seek to understand the place of the schools in the community by interviewing community partners as well as the staff of at least one social service agency that works as a partner with children in the school setting.

The discomfort of teacher education students in exploring these new and different partnerships is quite evident. It forces students to move beyond a classroom in which they are quite comfortable into a community chosen because of its diversity which is often quite different from the one in which the Maryville student grew up. But the students report, share, and come to understand the necessary conditions for partners in a community to support each other.

Can a street be a partner?

Finally, schools are explored as partners in a larger context in what has become known as "the street project." In order to help our students explore the need for partnerships in the metropolitan area, they are engaged in a semester long project with three of their cadre. Choosing from among about 12 streets that stretch from one end of the metropolitan area to the other, we ask them to examine the diversity of the community by exploring the economic, racial, cultural/ethnic, educational, architectural, religious and historical dimensions of the communities along the thoroughfare. By studying and presenting a critical analysis of the questions, problems and issues for the St. Louis community as exemplified by the street that they have studied, students begin to see the interconnections and complexities of the education of children in the entire community. In further studies, the students show evidence that education is broadly linked to partnerships in the entire community.

In their final synthesis, students often reflect with wonderment on their redefined beliefs and questions about the educational system and the role of teachers. They report that they understand that the connections of teachers with others in the school and the community are more related than they had expected.

Nature of partnerships

Do teacher education students intentionally think about issues of equity, access, and stewardship? Without redefining and attending to ongoing partnerships in schools and communities, we believe that the answer to the above question will be a disappointing "no." Partnerships focusing on common goals and points of view seem to produce results that provide simultaneous support and renewal for all partners. Each year of the partnerships described herein brings us to new questions as well as solutions. The next task for the partnerships described herein will be to better restructure our roles and time to spend even more time working on our efforts to educate children and teacher educators together. Linkages across partner schools are beginning to be formed around common problems. School-based faculty see teacher education students and teacher education faculty spending even more time in the schools. At this point, the possibilities are more likely to come to fruition because of the commitment of partners around a commonly focused agenda.

References

Duckworth, E. (1987). *The having of wonderful ideas and other essays on teaching and learning*. New York: Teachers College Press.

Feiman-Nemser, S. & Melnick, S. (1992). Introducing teaching. In Feiman-Nemser, S. & Featherstone, H. (Eds). *Exploring teaching: reinventing an introductory course*. New York: Teachers College Press.

Finch, M.E. (1995). *Becoming a reflective practitioner*. St. Louis: Maryville University.

Fosnot, C.T. (1989). *Enquiring teachers, enquiring learners: a constructivist approach for teaching*. New York: Teachers College Press.

Goodlad, J. I. (1994). *Educational renewal*. San Francisco: Jossey-Bass.

Goodlad, J.I. (1993). *Teachers for our nation's schools*. San Francisco: Jossey-Bass.

Rasch, K.D. (1990). Reflection in teacher preparation: A case study in program design. *Proceedings of the Third National Forum, AILACTE*, November 1990.

Working Together Year-Round: A Teaching-Training Partnership

Joseph D. Brown, Jimmie Russell, Judy Taylor Michael Lackey, Betty Chancellor

Oklahoma Baptist University

B
eginning in the fall of 1993, the Division of Teacher Education at Oklahoma Baptist University (OBU) and the North Rock Creek (NRC) Public Schools have had an ongoing partnership for providing remedial and enrichment classes during NRC's twice yearly intersessions. The partnership started after the Superintendent from NRC approached the Chair of OBU's Teacher Education Division asking for help in maintaining their intersession program. At the same time, OBU's education faculty were looking to develop a large on-going project with a local school district that was interdisciplinary and would allow the involvement of all teacher education students. Before the relationship began, a joint agreement outlining the services NRC and OBU students and faculty would provide for each other was developed by the NRC School Board and the OBU Division of Teacher Education and signed by both parties.

OBU is a senior-level coeducational liberal arts institution with an enrollment of approximately 2,450 students. It is owned and supported by the Baptist General Convention of Oklahoma. The Division of Teacher Education is accredited by the Oklahoma State Department of Education and the National Council for the Accreditation of Teacher Education.

NRC School's uniqueness comes from its being the only year-round school district in Oklahoma. Their academic calendar is a 45/10 cycle. The student population is comprised of approximately 55% white, 40% Native American, and 5% African American and Hispanic. More than 50% of the students are eligible for free or reduced breakfast and lunch. The district exceeds the state averages in percentage of students served in special education classes, Title 1 (Chapter 1) remedial reading classes, and in the number of students who are identified and served as limited English proficient (LEP) students. Yet, the district also exceeds the state averages in the percentage of students identified and served as gifted and talented.

At the present time, Oklahoma school districts receive funding for 180 academic days. Consequently, any extra teaching days provided by a district are paid from local funds or outside sources. Certified personnel at NRC are not required to teach during the intersessions, however, if they choose to participate they are compensated by the district for the extra days based on their average daily salary. NRC parents, teachers, administrators and school board members are convinced the benefits of an intersession far out weigh the extra cost. Therefore, by providing intersession teachers who are compensated with course credit, OBU helps reduce the amount of funding spent by NRC for intersession. This partnership, however, is not just about saving the district money. With total local control and OBU's status as a private institution, the partnership has not been encumbered by the usual litany of governmental requirements. As a result, it has been very easy to make changes and to try new ideas and methods.

Prior to the beginning of OBU's fall and spring semester, OBU teacher education and NRC faculty meet to confirm dates and deadlines for the upcoming intersession. Once the dates are established NRC faculty provide an orientation for OBU students explaining year-round education and the benefits the district hopes to provide for NRC students attending an intersession. OBU teacher education students, through their methodology classes, then design proposals for teaching enrichment or remedial classes during the intersession. The proposals must have learning objectives, a materials/equipment list, and an imaginative flier for advertising the course. Course proposals are reviewed by both OBU and North Rock Creek faculty prior to being accepted. Once accepted, the flier is put into a catalog that is sent home to the parents/guardians of the North Rock Creek students. Students and parents then decide in which activities to enroll. Each intersession has repeat classes, based on popularity and demand, from other sessions but also includes new classes designed around a new theme/topic. Enrollment in intersession classes is not required and students have the option of attending either morning, afternoon or all day. Presently, 85% of the NRC student body participate in intersession. Bus and food service is available on the same schedule as a regular school day.

OBU education students are allowed to work together in groups of two or three. This helps university students avoid having to miss other classes while at NRC. OBU students are afforded the opportunity to teach in more than one intersession week if they so choose. Therefore, during one intersession they could teach a math enrichment class and the next intersession teach an art class. Before their student teaching semester, teacher education students have the opportunity to participate in up to five intersessions.

Intersession classes are limited to no more than 11 students per instructor. Registration for remedial classes is limited to a maximum of three with a preferred ratio of one-to-one. NRC students needing mathematics and/or reading remediation are given a pre-test prior to intersession and a post-test following the intersession. Once the pre-test is completed, OBU students, teaching remediation courses, meet with NRC faculty to discuss pre-test results to help in planning for the child's particular need.

An evaluation form that was created jointly by OBU and North Rock Creek faculty and administration is used to assess the OBU education students' performance. The form includes items such as interaction with students, classroom control, preparedness, and following school policies. These areas are rated using a Likert Scale of 1 to 3, and a section for written comments by the evaluator is included on the document. Additional input is received from the NRC administrators, staff, OBU faculty, and parents of children attending intersession. Correspondingly, OBU education students are given the opportunity to express their likes and dislikes along with any suggestions and ideas they might have for improving the programs. No grades are issued for any intersession class; however, in some instances certificates of completion are given when warranted. Without the stress of grading, NRC students appear to be more willing to try new activities and to reattempt previous activities they had performed with poor success.

This alliance has allowed OBU students many opportunities such as hands-on learning before they student teach, working and planning with peers, flexibility in choosing activities, interaction with master teachers, receiving feedback on their teaching from someone other than university faculty, organizing time and materials, working in an "real" school environment, developing classroom management expertise in a controlled setting and working with an diverse ethnic student population. The result is OBU students with self-confidence in their teaching capability and a greater appreciation of the work it takes to create a learning opportunity. Many OBU students who teach an intersession request that they be placed at NRC for their 12-week student teaching assignment.

NRC students benefit from having a break from the usually rigid schedule and being allowed to explore their own interests in greater depth. It also affords NRC students exposure and interaction with adults who have empathy for their problems because of a closer age span and who are not parents or regular teachers. Those students who need remediation receive it after only 45 days and before the student becomes completely frustrated. The remediation, most times, is one which is not available during the regular sessions. Likewise, NRC students have the advantage of seeing the same material presented through a different approach which can be a key to skill development.

The NRC and OBU intersession partnership demonstrates, once again, that private higher education institutions can work with public schools. Since its inception, NRC and OBU have made presentations at national, regional, and state conferences about the intersession partnership. Consequently, three universities have developed similar arrangements with year-round public school districts in their area. At the present time, OBU and NRC are beginning their third year of partnership and have agreed to make this an ongoing project between the two institutions.

Sowing Seeds of Transformation: Partnerships with a Purpose

Shannon Clarkson

Quinnipiac College (Connecticut)

Transformation is a serious, timely endeavor akin to reformation, though perhaps without engendering the fear often associated with the latter. Reformation casts doubt on the present system, as reformers call forth a re-forming of current practice. Transformation implies change as well, but change which moves from the present into the future in a more graceful manner. The question for transformers is how to attain that grace so that change emerges as the opening of a flower, rather than through a grafting process or by pulling the old system up by the roots. The solution being designed at Quinnipiac College in Hamden, Connecticut, is emerging through a careful development and nourishment of partnerships in education.

The Master of Arts in Teaching (M.A.T.) program at Quinnipiac began in 1989 as an institutionally-based program only. Local school districts were involved only at the point of the student teaching experience in the students' education. Three years later, this isolationist position began to change. First the Internship and then the Residency portions of the M.A.T. program were developed as cooperative efforts among ten school districts in Connecticut. The vision in 1992 when these programs were initiated was multilayered: to create a program which would involve local school districts in a way that would lead to effective teacher education; to provide enrichment for area public school teachers and administrators; to enable the college faculty to learn and grow through their participation with graduate students and educational practitioners; and to provide educational and economic opportunities for M.A.T. students. Three years later, in 1995, a multi-faceted program has emerged which offers middle grades, secondary, and dual certification licenses. The partnerships have developed in the two ways named above: internship and residency. The first offers middle grades certification and takes thirteen months, the second is for either high school or middle grades and takes nineteen months.

Those in the middle grades residency program work in pairs, and through negotiations with local schools arranged by our staff, "replace" one teacher for the year and function as the fifth and sixth persons on a four-person team. Their time at Quinnipiac begins in June and runs through July of the following year, with their student teaching being incorporated into the residency experience. The Bridgeport teams increased the average math scores of their students to the equvalence of scores by students in the magnet school in the same town. Those in the internship also begin in June, but conclude their program with twelve weeks of student teaching the fall of their second year. Each year between thirty and forty students are placed in year-long internships at schools in eight districts in urban and suburban towns around the college. Both high schools and middle schools are included in the program.

The internship entered its fourth year in September 1995. Most of the districts have been with the program since its inception; two are newer. The intent is multifaceted: to offer students the opportunity to experience an entire school year in the public school, to enable the students to waive the tuition fees for two semesters, and to enable students the opportunity to experience both the high school and middle school environment. The partnership concept of both the internship and the residency has continued to evolve, notwithstanding some administrative turnover both in the district schools and in the college program. Principals are beginning to realize they play an important role in the success of the endeavor. Teachers, too, who serve as Advisors for the interns, have learned that if they are interested in becoming more involved with the teacher preparation program at the college, they may find themselves teaching a methods course in their discipline, developing an educational technologies course, or serving on an advisory committee.

While we have a contractual agreement with each school district, an effective partnership goes beyond signatures and "legalese." Time and a commitment to work together to create open lines of communication for the benefit of all parties are vital ingredients of any successful partnership. Each year we learn more about how to nurture the students in our program as well as the teachers and administrators in the schools who are all critical to the educational task. After the "advisors' tea" last spring, the consensus from the interns and advisors was that the next such event should include a more formal program. Consequently, this year a panel of former advisors and interns will talk about their experiences with the new advisors. And each year, the teachers and administrators with whom we work have begun increasingly to "own" their participation in our efforts. The 1994-95 interns helped to create a set of guidelines for those involved with us. These proposed guidelines were then shared with the administrators in each school with which we work and modified with their clarifications. This year, those modified guidelines were given to the new interns and sent to their Advisors and to the administrators who helped to formulate them. Consequently, arrangements which were originally created by the college alone have now been amended by those most involved in the day-to-day life of the program: the students and school administrators.

With a full-time staff of one administrator and two faculty members, the size of our program has certain parameters. One important delimiter is determined simply by the hours in a day. To maintain and strengthen relationships among the schools, their district offices, and the college, the faculty coordinator must be in contact with them. Maximum contractual placement in the ten districts totals fifty-eight full time students: sixteen in the residency program and forty-two in internships. Were we to increase the number of students by increasing the districts involved, more staff would be needed. A small, well-connected program runs the danger of form exceeding function if the very connections on which the program flourishes are stretched beyond their capacity, or worse, neglected. Effective partnerships require personal interactions among the participants, not just careful administrative detail.

The last stage in the transformation process in which we have engaged is just now beginning to emerge. Transforming schools from within requires a commitment on the part of staff to work for change, yet oftentimes long-time staff members are reluctant to modify their methods or attitudes. New teachers, whose educational experience has exposed them to new forms of assessment, portfolio development, interdisciplinary teaching, and inclusive classrooms, are eager to put their new theories into practice. The hope for the M.A.T. partnership at Quinnipiac is that as more of our students are hired by our partner schools, more possibilities will arise for school transformation.

For example, one area middle school hired a teacher from our first graduating class four years ago. Last year she was the advisor for one of our interns. This summer, two former interns in the high school in that district were hired as middle school teachers. Another student is doing his student teaching there this semester and two more are interns for the year. The two who have recently been hired are pleased that they have each other for support. Moves toward heterogeneous grouping meet resistance among most of the faculty. Monthly "mapping" strategies by the principal to encourage interdisciplinary lesson planning are not taken very seriously, and few have signed up to try alternative methods of assessment.

Yet some teachers are willing to follow along with the new ideas. One of last year's interns worked in the middle school's summer school program with the computer lab teacher. The teacher wanted to teach various writing styles using a class newspaper as the medium. Kevin suggested that they use the computer simulation game, "Sim City," to both introduce computer skills and to provide students with material for their newspaper. Although a bit skeptical at first, the teacher agreed and the students' work showed they were learning the skills and interest was high. In his student teaching experience this fall, Kevin has convinced his cooperating teacher to let him try a three-week unit on Egypt which Kevin plans to teach in the computer lab. If the unit is successful, Kevin has discussed with the cooperating teacher how the unit may be taught in other years using other historical periods.

Carol, one of the two Quinnipiac former interns hired at the middle school this year, reports that some of the teachers have expressed concerns to her about the new middle grades credential. Because the middle grades credential is new to the state of Connecticut, few teachers have that particular certification, even though they may be teaching in a middle grades context. The next step the Quinnipiac M.A.T. program plans to take, is to offer middle grades certification preparation for those already teaching in that area. This year, several middle grades teachers who teach in our program are working with Mary McKenna, the other faculty on our staff, and Carol Orticari, the director, to develop such a program. Were this to come about, the teachers who have indicated their anxiety might find that anxiety relieved by participating in these new classes at Quinnipiac.

The newest seed germinating in our partnership is still in the planning stages as well. Our graduates with teaching positions in area schools tell us they would benefit from periodic colloquia focused on current issues in education. They are anxious for a time to meet with each other and other interested teachers and share the joys and frustrations of life "in the field." The plans are for a group of graduates to work with the M.A.T. staff to develop a yearly series, to which alums and teachers in our partnership would be invited.

To profess to being agents of transformation necessitates that we ourselves be open for transformation. Working in a collaborative way with area schools and with the needs and requests of the state board of education also brings with it the concomitant need to be flexible. Each district is different, as is each school within each district. Yet a philosophy of education that prefers quality to quantity and human relationships to rules gives guidance and direction to a program seeking to develop excellent teachers through the partnership process.

Running with the River: A Partnership Project Involving An Integrated Curriculum

Natalie Abell, Melissa Cain, Elizabeth Raker

University of Findlay (Ohio)

Project Overview

In 1992, teacher education faculty at The University of Findlay made a commitment to actively pursue curricula that view communication and multimedia technologies as indispensable tools facilitating interdisciplinary learning. This was based on the belief that fostering the development of children, both educationally and socially, is critical to the future of our global society. The future will demand that our children develop abilities to communicate effectively, access knowledge, think critically, and solve problems. Communications, data gathering, and decision making will occur at quicker rates than in the past. Technology will play an even greater role. Children are ready and eager to accept the challenge. Their teachers must be prepared to guide them. Teacher education programs that meet the needs of the future will be those that have vision, determination, and the ability to effect systemic change.

With these goals in mind, Teacher Education at The University of Findlay, in collaboration with Findlay City Schools and Putnam County Schools, submitted a winning proposal to Ameritech. The ensuing program, "Running with the River: Collaboration Through Technology," involves the development and implementation of both preservice and inservice teacher training programs that seamlessly integrate state-of-the-art communications and multimedia technologies into the academic curricula of the university and the public schools. Reconceptualization of the university and public school curricula center around an integrated thematic program of study focusing on water: the Blanchard River flows

151

through Hancock and Putnam Counties as a tributary of the Great Lakes Watershed.

Phase I, Development and Training, took place from March to September 1994. It focused on establishing network communications capabilities, selecting participants, and orienting participants to the project. Also included were development and implementation of inservice for university Teacher Education faculty and public school teachers, as well as curriculum development on both the university and K-12 level.

Mentor teachers were selected from a pool of teachers from the Findlay City and Putnam County Schools who expressed an interest and were recommended by their administration. Mentor-teacher teams from seven schools in Findlay and five schools in Putnam County participated. The University of Findlay partnered Teacher Education juniors with the mentor-teacher teams. Each teacher was given an Apple PowerBook portable computer to use throughout the year.

During this first phase, a Project Director with a Ph.D. in Educational Technology was hired to coordinate daily project activities and to provide instruction and guidance in communications and multimedia technologies. A Network Manager was also hired to ensure smooth setup and operation of the technology portion of the project in both the university setting and in the public schools. Summer work sessions allowed public school teachers and university faculty to restructure their respective curricula in preparation for fall implementation. Participants (teachers, university students and faculty) were introduced to the World Wide Web as a means of communication, data sharing, and conferencing with others interested in monitoring water quality of rivers both nationally (specifically, the Great Lakes) and internationally.

Phase II, Curriculum Implementation, began in September 1994. Mentor-teacher/ university junior teams are implementing the thematic water project. Children in grades 3-11 are participating in thematic units studying the water quality of the Blanchard River and other water-related topics. Collected information is shared within their class, among buildings in the same district via fiber optics, and between students in the two school systems via Internet.

Major Outcomes of the Project

- Comprehensive integration of communication and multimedia technologies across undergraduate teacher education programs at The University of Findlay and across elementary and secondary curricula of the Findlay City and Putnam County Schools;

- Development of technology-based, integrated thematic curricula providing a reality-based, active learning environment;

- Development of a permanent technologies mentorship program, partnering select teachers from the Findlay City and Putnam County Schools with Teacher Education juniors from The University of Findlay;

- Establishment of ongoing educational communication links among The University of Findlay, Findlay City and Putnam County Schools, and the broader educational community.

Specific Objectives of the Project

- Provide university teacher education faculty and K-12 teachers the necessary skills, expertise and support to integrate communications and multimedia technologies into their courses and methodologies;

- Support the mentorship teams, as well as public school building administrators, as they develop strategies, methods and materials that recognize technology as a critical learning tool;

- Foster communication, peer support and on-going learning by utilizing a topical on-line forum;

- Create a lending library of technology equipment essential for implementation of the communications technology curriculum in the mentor teacher classrooms;

- Initiate an ongoing graduate level summer institute which blends new technologies and thematic academic content with a focus on community-based research;

- Develop in Teacher Education juniors, K-12 children, and their teachers critical thinking and problem-solving skills;

- Evaluate effectiveness of a technology integrated curriculum in a teacher training program;

- Contribute Blanchard River water quality data to The Great Lakes River Basin Project;

- Share knowledge, strategies, skills gained by participants in the project with the broader educational community.

Beyond the two year funding period, the project will have established an ongoing undergraduate curricular framework of technology integration, mentorship, and communicative collaboration among a consortium of three progressive educational entities in Northwest Ohio. Within this new framework, countless other thematic academic areas can be studied

153

(e.g., air quality, recycling, political elections) collaboratively among the three entities, utilizing the communication technologies piloted during the project. The lending library of technology equipment will support the continuation of this collaborative curricula beyond the Ameritech funding. Additionally, the expertise developed by the three entities during the funding years will allow for extension of the project through a Summer Institute offering workshops and seminars for practicing teachers throughout the region. Future institutes will focus on graduate study in communications and multimedia technologies leadership, but always within the context of an academic theme.

Methods Component

The junior year Teacher Education curriculum at The University of Findlay was restructured during the 1994-95 school year, clustering the methods courses to reflect the integrated, thematic approach being implemented in the public schools. This involved the integrated teaching of Science Methods, Social Studies Methods, and Children's Literature. The Science Methods teacher is Mr. Ron Bowerman, a science teacher at Donnell Middle School in Findlay. The Social Studies Methods instructor is Elizabeth Raker and the Children's Literature instructor is Melissa Cain, both University of Findlay faculty.

The team met during the summer to define the parameters of the integrated teaching of the three disciplines. Although the subject areas enhanced each other, each had a unique set of essential knowledge and skills; so some individual subject meetings were necessary. Methodology, however, cut across subject constraints. Team and individual meetings both incorporated cooperative learning and multiple intelligences activities. Subthemes related to water were selected, as well as related pieces of children's literature, which would be one focus for the activities. Juniors were also required to incorporate cooperative learning and multiple intelligences in their planning for the public school children.

There was no theme for the first team meeting with the university juniors. The evening was devoted to an explanation of course expectations. The lesson plan format developed by Teacher Education faculty was discussed. Cooperative learning materials, which came from a Spencer Kagan workshop and the Northwest Ohio Regional Teacher Training Center, were distributed. Material on multiple intelligences came from a David Lazear workshop at the Findlay City Schools. Graphic organizers specific to the disciplines were developed to facilitate planning lessons to include all of the seven intelligences: Visual-Spatial, Verbal Linguistic, Logical-Mathematical, Body-Kinesthetic, Interpersonal, Intrapersonal, and Musical. An additional thrust of lesson planning was making sure the lesson took students beyond the knowledge level. Handouts to juniors included several with questions to ask when planning for multiple intelligences and higher-order thinking. Several water-related experiences demonstrated these combined instructional strategies. As an example, after listening to The Water of Life, a folk tale retold by Barbara Rogasky, juniors completed a related cooperative learning activity, Numbered Heads Together. This focused on knowledge-level questioning. They then worked in cooperative groups to write questions that would cause students to think about the book beyond the knowledge level.

The first theme was Wetlands/Wildlife. A field trip to Maumee Bay State Park provided first-hand experience with the wetland environment. The university juniors and faculty explored the wetlands on an extensive boardwalk tour of lakefront wetland areas. They examined flora and fauna and took QuickTake pictures and video recordings of their experiences. They met with the park naturalist, who gave them an overview of the importance of conserving area wetlands. Students then participated in an orienteering activity using compasses. Upon their return to the university, they formulated a newsletter incorporating their QuickTake pictures.

The second theme was Native Americans. The connection to the theme "Running with the River" was that natives and early settlers in Findlay/Putnam County were dependent upon the Blanchard River for many things. Related children's literature was Elizabeth George Speare's *Sign of the Beaver* and Joan Blos's *Brothers of the Heart*. These acted as illustrations of what it would be like to live in a wilderness area and of the relationships that developed between natives and settlers. Bowerman is an expert on local history and native groups and has many artifacts that he shared with the juniors. A Toledo resident, Joyce Mahaney, President of the Intertribal Council, came and spoke about growing up on her reservation and about the sensitivities teachers should have to native cultures. QuickTake pictures of Mrs. Mahaney were put into a HyperStudio stack of the concepts of her talk.

Mapping exercises with *The Sign of the Beaver* and *Brothers of the Heart* were done for social studies. A Spencer Kagan Spin 'n Think cooperative learning activity focused students on the literary elements related to the two books. In-class development of additional Spin 'n Think cards allowed the juniors to develop additional activities they could use in their field experience classrooms. Multiple intelligence planning charts were used to brainstorm multiple intelligence activities for *The Sign of the Beaver*. A final speaker was Rick Carles, an archeologist, who shared many artifacts from local archaeological digs. Dis-

cussion followed about the controversies that can arise between archae-
ologists and native peoples over repatriotization of artifacts.

A third theme, introduced spring semester, was weather. Bowerman
demonstrated laser disc technology with this theme. There was no
specific children's book for this theme. Rather, the juniors explored a
variety of books related to the theme and selected those that would
enhance the unit they were planning with their mentor teachers. Team
time was taken to share and assess progress on lesson/unit plan development. Assessment was according to scoring criteria which were
distributed when the assignment was given. Included in the criteria
were inclusion of various levels of technology, cooperative learning, and
multiple intelligences; accommodation for cultural diversity and students with special needs; and promotion of thinking beyond the knowledge level.

The final theme was water quality. Natalie Babbitt's *The Search for
Delicious* was used to demonstrate a comprehension grid activity, which
is a literature-based reading strategy. *The Search for Delicious* is a
fantasy about a mythical kingdom in which a young man undertakes a
quest to find a suitable dictionary definition for "delicious." When an
evil lord turns off the kingdom's water source, everyone agrees that
"water" is the definition for "delicious." This book was a good example
of how fantasy can speak to real world issues and nicely balanced the
juniors' own investigations of water quality in the Blanchard River
carried out in Science Methods.

Other Science Methods classes were held at a local park, Oakwoods,
which is partly a wetland environment. There, monitoring of the wetland was done through probes and computers set up by Mr. Bowerman.
Additionally, the juniors were trained to teach with Project Wet, Project
Wild, Project Learning Tree, and the Leopold Education Project. All of
these are resources for hands-on, thematic teaching of science concepts.
The Leopold Education Project centers on the work of Aldo Leopold, an
early conservationist. His *Sand County Almanac* was used as an
illustration of literature based upon observation of the natural environment. Mirroring this, juniors kept careful records of their own observations of the growth of several "adopted" buds.

Coordinated with the Ohio Social Studies Core Curriculum, the
Social Studies Methods classes explored the major areas of elementary
social studies: history, geography, economics, civics, and citizenship
participation. Through a systematic program of interactive activities,
students examined, evaluated, and responded to a variety of social
studies curricula and methodologies. Students worked in cooperative
groups practicing lesson plans involving multiple intelligences, higher-
order thinking skills, and group problem-solving strategies. Current

social studies trends were discussed and critiqued. Emphasis was placed on the development of cross-disciplinary links with language arts and science, including technology enhancements.

The purpose of the Survey of Children's Literature is to expose preservice teachers to the wide variety of children's literature that is available today. Part of the course is the study of the various genre and the literary elements, as well as the techniques of questioning and discussion and the application of children's literature to the teaching of reading and language arts. Individual class nights were needed because the theme of water couldn't cover the whole spectrum of children's literature. However, as part of the class, students helped annotate an extensive bibliography of children's books on the theme of water. This was done in the Macintosh Lab and consolidated to be put on the project's World Wide Web Home Page (http://river@findlay.edu). Students also used the Macintosh Lab to explore a variety of interactive children's books on CD and several story writing programs, notably MECC's Storybook Weaver. Additionally, students explored the children's literature resources available on the Internet.

Technology Integration

The project was supported by technology-rich learning opportunities for all involved. Technology was viewed as a tool for research, writing or personal management; developing learning activities and collaborative products; planning assessment and instruction; and communication beyond individual settings. Technology training was addressed in several systematic levels. First, mentors/juniors practiced technology skills that enabled them to efficiently perform their own work in terms of personal and professional organization and management. For example, they learned word processing to develop lesson plans, parent letters, report forms, etc. Data bases and spreadsheets were used for grading, mail merging, and sorting for various purposes. The second level involved using technology tools to present instruction. Lower level technologies included overheads, video, and cassette recordings. Higher level technologies included laser disc, LCD panels, QuickTake cameras, and computers. The third level provided opportunities for the public school children to use technology to research and solve problems. Examples were CD Rom, laser discs, simulations, data bases, electronic encyclopedias, fiber optics, email, and the Internet. The final level allowed the juniors and K-12 students to produce and present their own work using computers, scanners, printers, LCD panels, video production, and QuickTake cameras.

A series of four technology mini-conferences or workshops occurred throughout the juniors' program of study. Mentor teachers were encouraged to attend alongside their university partners. These workshops allowed them to interact with professionals outside of the local area as they expanded their technology knowledge base. University juniors brought laptop computers and video cameras to their mentor-teacher sites, using the equipment throughout the year to support instruction. Computers were used by mentor-teachers, juniors and children for data collection at the Blanchard River, data analysis and presentation, project/product development, and communication with the public schools using email and the Internet. During the summer months, the lending library of technological equipment was returned to the university to support the Summer Institute and other teacher inservice.

Technology was interwoven into the individual methods courses and team nights. Students used the PowerBooks that were assigned to them for the year to prepare electronic journals of their professional response to the events of each class meeting. These were turned in on disk and read by the methods team, who entered responses directly on each disk. The theme of the Teacher Education program at The University of Findlay is "Reflective Practitioners in a Climate of Change." Electronic journals were a great way to enable students to reflect upon their learning and for instructors to monitor and respond to their thinking.

The highest level of technology used in the project was fiber optics. The Fiber Optics Lab at The University of Findlay was designed for optimum flexibility. Computer connections and other electronics are located in floor boxes, allowing tables to be moved into a variety of arrangements. The room is equipped with video cameras that can be preset to different positions. There is a bank of four large television monitors. Three additional monitors occupy the remaining corners of the room, so that a monitor can be easily seen from anywhere in the room. Elmo, a video camera, is mounted to point down at a document or three dimensional object, which can then be shown on the monitors. Elmo is a wonderful tool for sharing. The camera can zoom in and out so that even tiny objects or parts of pictures can become the focus for discussion. Beyond high tech "show and tell," the Fiber Optics Lab could link to the seven existing fiber optics rooms in the Findlay City Schools. In this way, the university juniors could interact with children in the public schools without physically leaving the campus.

An example of fiber optics in action took place when Ohio's governor, George V. Voinovich, and Ameritech Ohio's president, Jacqueline F. Woods, visited The University of Findlay for a demonstration. For this event, the Fiber Optics Lab at The University of Findlay was linked to the one at Donnell Middle School. Mr. Bowerman and his middle school students have created three mini-biomes outside his classroom. The middle school students set up a remote camera at one of the biomes, a pond. Through fiber optics, they were able to share with the audience located at The University of Findlay what they had learned about the pond environment. Then, three university juniors presented additional information about pond environments all over the world to the middle school students. During the presentations, participants were able to interact with one another as if they were in the same room. A highlight for the middle school students was being able to talk to the governor about his experiences with ponds and about School Net, his plan to electronically link every school in Ohio.

The final project for the juniors was an integrated unit related to the theme of water. The units were developed with mentor teachers and "field tested" in the mentor teacher's classrooms. Each unit was required to follow the lesson plan format adopted by Teacher Education; integrate social studies, science, and children's literature; incorporate cooperative learning and multiple intelligence activities; accommodate for children with special needs, including diverse cultures; and cause children to think beyond the knowledge level. Both high and low level technology components were integrated into the unit plans. A wide variety of projects resulted. One focused on the history of mills in the area. One traced the source of water for the City of Findlay. Another was on frog dissection. The high school students monitored water quality and exchanged information via email. Another team developed a video of a historical timeline of events which occurred along the Blanchard River. Alternative assessments were emphasized as an important aspect of lesson/unit planning. Instructors modeled this by clearly defining assessment criteria for the units, which were distributed to students to aid them in their planning.

Conclusion

During the first year of "Running with the River: Collaboration Through Technology," substantial achievements were realized. A public school mentorship program was established between The University of Findlay and the Putnam County and Findlay City Schools. Extensive integration of technology within targeted courses at The University of Findlay and the public schools has occurred. Formative evaluation of the process indicates that the project has been successful in meeting the proposed project objectives. Formative evaluation data have been incorporated in the planning for the second year of "Running of the River: Collaboration through Technology." The impact of the project on teaching and learning is reflected in the comments of Sue Becker, an inter-disciplinary art teacher at Central Middle School:

> I feel so lucky to have been a part of this project, which has been a renewal to my teaching . . . To be able to offer kids a chance to research information in a way that they are so "turned on to" makes teaching exciting again. I love to teach but you can burn out so easily from all of the issues that filter into our jobs. It was great to have students and teachers excited, knowing that we are on the cutting edge of technology in our classroom.

Resources

American Forest Foundation. (1994). *Project Learning Tree: Environmental education activity guide (Pre K-8).* Washington, D.C.: American Forest Foundation.

Babbitt, N. (1990). *The search for delicious.* New York: Farrar, Straus, & Giroux.

Blos, J. (1987). *Brothers of the heart.* New York: Macmillan.

Kagan, S. (1992). *Cooperative learning.* San Juan Capistrano, CA: Kagan Cooperative Learning.

Lazear, D. G. *Teaching for, with, and about multiple intelligences.* Chicago, IL: New Dimensions of Learning.

Leopold, A. (1968). *A Sand County Almanac.* New York: Oxford University Press.

Martorella, P. H. (1994). *Social studies for elementary school children: Developing young citizens.* New York: Merrill.

MECC. (1993). *Storybook weaver.* Minneapolis, MN: MECC.

Pheasants Forever. (1992). *The Leopold Education Project: Lessons in a land ethic.* St. Paul, MN: Pheasants Forever, Inc.

Rogasky, B. (1986). *The water of life.* Illustrated by Trina Schart Hyman. New York: Holiday House.

Rothlein, L. and A. M. Meinbach. (1991). *The literature connection.* Glenview, IL: Good Year Books.

Speare, E. G. (1984). *Sign of the beaver.* New York: Dell.

The Watercourse and Western Regional Environmental Education Council. (1995). *Project WET: Curriculum and activity guide.* Houston, TX: Western Regional Environmental Education Council and Bozeman, MT: The Watercourse.

Western Regional Environmental Education Council. (1992). Project WILD. Bethesda, MD: Western Regional Environmental Education Council.

Race, Culture and Power: A Collaborative Approach In Diversity Training and Educational Reform

Richard L. Biffle

Willamette University (Oregon)

T he changing ethnic face of today's society has brought growing cultural diversity to our workplace, schools and community. Throughout these institutions, effective communication across cultures is the key to establishing good relationships for productive teaching and instruction. To this date, the ability to harness the strengths of diversity, develop the vital communication and instructional skills, and solve these institutional challenges remain underdeveloped. Schools typically are not well prepared to deal with the range of unique needs associated with an increasing population of culturally- and language-diverse students. A parallel pressed upon public schools is the effort to effect educational reform and improvement through a variety of policy changes.

This chapter will discuss a unique curricular partnership between the Willamette University School of Education and the Salem-Keizer School District SMART (Salem-Keizer Multicultural Resource Team) advisory group in Salem, Oregon, as both institutions strengthen the capabilities of student teachers and teacher educators in meeting and maximizing the challenges and opportunities of cultural diversity. The article will provide the essential foundation for understanding the interrelationship of culture and instructional practice and their impact on preservice education programs as related to each institution's overall mission and goals.

Why is This Necessary Anyway?

The issues and challenges surrounding multicultural education and cultural pluralism refuse to go away. The teaching profession is once again on the frontline of the struggle, but we are faced with the unsettling discovery that many of our newly "minted" teachers are ill-equipped to deal the complexities of issues related to ethnic or cultural diversity. As James Banks (1994) states in his book *An Introduction to Multicultural Education:*

> Education within a pluralistic society should affirm and help students understand their home and community cultures. However, it should also help free them from their cultural boundaries. To create and maintain a civic community that works for the common good, education in a democratic society should help students acquire the knowledge, attitudes, and skills they will need to participate in civic action to make society more equitable and just. (p. 1)

In order to better understand the various roles that teacher education programs must play in helping student teachers navigate these precarious waters of the time, we must begin to re-evaluate the mission and nature of preservice training programs. A critical area that needs re-examination or reorganization is multicultural education training, in addition to the types of experiences students are engaged in during programs, courses, or workshops.

It is simply not enough to prepare professional educators in a manner that addresses only pedagogy, evaluation and assessment methods, and curriculum and instructional strategies. Serious efforts in the area of multicultural educational training, experiences that will be of invaluable assistance to new teachers who are being assigned to increasingly diverse classrooms and school environments, must be included as an integral part of any preservice education program. This training should include collaborative and cooperative experiences between the university and school districts/sites in which student teachers are assigned. In addition, activities need to be designed that strengthen the capabilities of educators to meet and maximize the challenges and opportunities of cultural diversity. These activities provide the essential foundation for understanding the interrelationship of culture and instructional practice and their impact on schools and classrooms.

Finding the Missing Link . . .

Traditionally, preservice training in the area of multicultural education has involved a series of approaches ranging from survey or introductory activities to immersion experiences (with many programs focusing on the survey or introductory approach). Depending on the teacher education program philosophy, mission statement, goals or curriculum content these experiences may or may not assist the preservice teacher in developing a comprehensive understanding of culture or in being able to apply what has been learned to an educational setting. Well meaning desires to expand knowledge and understanding of multicultural education in this instance have often times digressed into course or training activities that address only issues related to celebrations of ethnic holidays, food and dress.

The problems inherent in this situation are by no means limited to preservice program activities at the university. They are a major cause of concern in school districts as well. Many successful multicultural education staff development and training programs have suffered tremendous setbacks because of poorly funded or poor organizational management practices that have "buried" these programs in low priority categories or isolated departments within the school district. Schools, administrators and classroom teachers are often left with "celebrations" because that is all that is left of once thriving and beneficial programs that created a sense of community and progress related to bringing together the total school community. With few or non-existent resources, the school or classroom teachers are often unable to go to the next level of development, knowledge or understanding—unless a creative approach is designed or identified to benefit both the school district/school site and the preservice teaching program.

Creating a Partnership: Common Needs and Interests

The function of preservice education and public education depends on the willingness of the constituent groups to develop a philosophy, goals and program objectives of education appropriate to the needs of their students and their respective communities within the context of a vastly changed and changing society. It should be recognized that the university and the school district must share accountability for quality public education. The education of children must be the shared responsibility of the university and the schools. Procedures should be incorporated which encourage trust and cooperation among the participants. A variety of methods, when used in combinations, can be helpful in establishing an environment of cooperative action. One such approach is a collaborative activity in preservice multicultural education training between Willamette University and the Salem-Keizer School District.

Multicultural education is an integral part of the preservice experience for all students enrolled in the Willamette University Master of Arts in Teaching (M.A.T.) Program and is part of the School of Education mission statement. The M.A.T. Program is a unique ten-month program that includes a year-long placement opportunity in public school classrooms. The commitment to multicultural education is outlined in the *School of Education Mission Statement and Goals* (1994):

> We are committed to the ideal that all students can and must learn regardless of differences. All students are persons of worth, deserving of respect and our best efforts on their behalf. The emphasis of the program is to enhance the capabilities of professional educators in the areas of educational leadership, collaboration, multicultural education, and educational technology.

An additional aspect of the program and the shared vision of the team is a strong commitment to multicultural education. This includes the preparation of MAT students who demonstrate the knowledge, skills and attitudes essential to addressing the changing needs and populations of the public schools. In addition to a Multicultural module in the core program, each instructor consciously includes attention to issues of multicultural education in both content and methodology.

We discovered that our mission statement and goals closely paralleled those of the Salem-Keizer School District, in which the majority of our preservice students are placed. The district is firmly committed to multicultural education action plans, known as School Climate Plans, at each school site and administrative department. Selected portions of the *Salem-Keizer School District Mission Statement and Goals* (1993) related to issues of multicultural education and diversity are highlighted as follows:

> In partnership with the community, we ensure that each student will have the essential knowledge, skills and attitudes to be a lifelong leaner, a contributing and productive worker in a changing and increasingly diverse world.

> We will focus all efforts to help each student develop the necessary knowledge and experiences to develop positive self-concept, respect for others, and healthy behavior patterns; demonstrate civic, global and environmental responsibility; recognize and value diversity among people.

> As an organization, the School District will treat people fairly and with equity; value and celebrate diversity among people of all cultures and abilities; refuse to tolerate racism, discrimination, harassment, and prejudice.

The identification of education needs requires a blending of university and school district missions and goals at times. The process should be an interesting investigative activity as to the possibilities for collaboration and cooperation, as well as an opportunity for expressing individual opinions. As a result of these and other activities, the task of discussing educational philosophy, identifying the needs of preservice or school district programs, determining mutual goals and objectives, and establishing priorities become essential elements in providing direction for further planning and action which will lead to authentic learning programs.

Weaving a New Tapestry of Multicultural Education Training

Multicultural education training in our preservice program at Willamette University is modular in design and uses a multicultural education method that was developed by James Banks. This method provides a firm theoretical and practical foundation for discussion, research, session activities and project designs. The workshop format enables students to be actively involved in a variety of experiences that can be implemented in their school classrooms or sites. Another benefit of this approach is that students can become an additional resource to supervising teachers and school sites in generating activities and programs related to multicultural education. Workshop session activities for students include "shadowing a student" experiences, small group projects, oral presentations and guest speakers. One of the more meaningful small group activities that students have enjoyed has been the design and creation of a School Climate Plan.

Briefly, the School Climate Plan was developed in 1992 by the Salem-Keizer School District in collaboration with several district committees and programs: the District School Climate Committee, Multicultural Education Programs Office, Equity Issues Committee and the Salem-Keizer School District Multicultural Advisory Resource Team. The overall purpose of the School Climate Plan is to ensure that significant progress toward implementation of the District's adopted mission and goals related to multicultural education and diversity is being made. This includes, but is not limited to, increasing multicultural education training and activities, and monitoring and review of the district mission statement and goals. Each school site, administrative department and support unit is required to design a specific plan of action addressing Multicultural Education that is comprehensive, well-coordinated, inclusive and integrated into the total philosophy of the school district. Overall monitoring and review of the plans are done by the District SMART Team which also provides technical assistance to sites. In accordance with district policy, each school or department climate plan must include the following tasks on their *Building School Climate Activities Plan* (1993):

- plan addressing issues of racism, discrimination, harassment and prejudice;

- recognize, expand, develop student efforts which are addressing racism, discrimination, harassment and prejudice;

- ensure opportunities for student, parent, staff, and community input into policies and practices;

- review LSAC (Local School Advisory Council) policies and membership to achieve racial diversity;

- enable school partnerships to flourish, not only within schools, but between schools, within areas and across areas;

- ensure that each School Improvement Team develops a multicultural plan for their school that includes involvement from staff, students and the community;

- expand ways to welcome new students at all levels;

- develop student body/student government sensitivity at student activities;

- review membership in student governance and student activities to encourage participation from all ethnic and cultural groups;

- survey student and staff regarding their awareness and sensitivity to racism and multicultural issues.

In a unique approach and experience, Willamette University pre-service students are involved in a multicultural education training activity that supports the local school district's efforts in designing, implementing and evaluating multicultural education plans and activities. Students are required, as part of their workshop session activities, to develop and write school climate plans using the school district guidelines and SMART Team assistance. This project has turned into an enjoyable collaborative and cooperative effort between student teachers and school district administrators, staffs, students, support personnel and community groups.

Projects are coordinated in design/planning teams which are made up of 4-6 students per team. A portion of the Bank's multicultural education model (1994) is used as a primary resource (specifically his *"Eight Characteristics of a Multicultural School"* and the *"Multicultural Curriculum Reform Approaches—Contributions, Additive, Transformation, and Social Action"*) for students in their initial deliberations and planning designs. During one of the first workshop sessions (there are six 2-hour training sessions in all) students are asked to evaluate actions taken in the district relative to multicultural education activities that have ensured that coordination and fulfillment of projected actions have or are taking place (based on information and resources available from the SMART Team and school district). The next step is for students to consider questions that are necessary in order to design, implement, and evaluate the progress of a school climate plan. These questions are:

1) What are the specific roles and responsibilities of district coordinators, advisory groups and committees, school site improvement teams, leadership teams, and area administrators?

2) What current efforts are being planned/implemented at this time relative to multicultural education by district areas and/or schools?

3) Who will be responsible for evaluating on-going and projected plans for multicultural education?

The process that design/planning teams follow is comprehensive and makes an important connection between multicultural education theory and application in an actual school setting or school environment. Students are required to present their plans not only in the final workshop session, but to their school site and SMART Team as well. The results of the student school climate plan designs was phenomenal! Students were able to identify and assess needs of schools, make connections between workshop session discussions and research, and develop plans that have been utilized throughout the district. Through a series of invaluable and "authentic experiences" (interviews with various educators/students/community people, compiling and synthesizing information, background research and supplemental readings, examination of curriculum and resource materials, identification of community resources, etc.) students began to develop some insights into how to meet the needs of school sites, departments and the school district as related to multicultural education programs and activities. Students also began to understand and appreciate the numerous challenges that schools and the district face when embarking upon changes to the existing structure, and their role as leaders in that process of change.

The School Climate Plan project is a "living document"—a plan that can be designed, implemented, evaluated and assessed in a number of ways. It is a collaborative effort between two educational institutions that recognize that learning and teaching are shared responsibilities—occurring at all times and affected by a multitude of influences. Pre-service students become empowered and take "ownership" of their plans in the following ways: (1) demonstrating that they can plan and design a comprehensive multicultural education plan—complete with evaluation and assessment procedures, (2) demonstrating that they can assess and make recommendations to various administrators about site concerns, problems, and needs, (3) identifying staff training needs and community resources, (4) developing knowledge and understanding of the critical importance related to monitoring and reviewing of plans, as well as timeline and scheduling management, (5) reviewing and examining of instructional materials and practices, (6) providing technical assistance to other educators, (7) and working cooperatively to appreciate the concerns of others as well as the will to overcome our mutual problems. School district personnel, students and community see the importance and expanding directions of the preservice education program in addition to witnessing student teacher participation in a broader and more meaningful context.

The open exchange of information and ideas is crucial to the success of a collaborative partnership. This one activity supports the notion that by identifying a few critical resources, coupled with engaging in creative thinking, a more meaningful learning experience is discovered by many audiences. Successful school-district-community planning in multicultural education is characterized by clearly stated purposes, good communication, high levels of cooperation and trust, and accepted leadership from a variety of sources. The ultimate goal of such planning is the synthesizing of the needs and aspirations of both communities into a plan for positive action. Successful preservice education programs must begin to identify the pressing need of today's students and judge how our programs can help meet them, particularly in the area of multicultural education. Many of the solutions and answers are close at hand—if we just take a little time to see what is available at or just outside our doors.

References

Banks, J. (1994). *Introduction to multicultural education*. Needham Heights, MA: Allyn and Bacon.

Salem-Keizer School District. (1993). *District mission and goals statement*. Salem, OR

Salem-Keizer School District. (1993). *School climate activities plan*. Salem, OR

School of Education, Willamette University. (1994). *Mission and goals statement*. Salem, OR

Collaborating for Partnerships in Science and Mathematics Education

Betty R. Tutt
Nancy Foley

William Woods University (Missouri)

Setting the Stage

In May 1993, against a backdrop of sweeping national educational reform, the Missouri legislature passed what is known to Missourians as the Outstanding Schools Act. The new law legislated, among other things, the development of rigorous academic performance standards, curriculum frameworks, and assessments. For practicing teachers, as well as teacher preparation institutions, this mandated reform necessitated a strengthened commitment to ensuring that all students, including those at risk for academic failure, meet high expectations.

Concomitantly with these statewide and national educational reforms, the Department of Education at William Woods University, a private, women-centered liberal arts institution in central Missouri, had been involved in several projects for educational renewal. These projects resulted in a variety of partnerships—some across various departments of the university, some with other educational entities, and others between the university and the local and county community. These partnerships included involvement in a RE:Learning consortium, the implementation of a school and community linkage project, the continuation of the university's annual special education conference, and the strengthening of the university's on-going mathematics and science education project with local school districts.

Science and Mathematics Are For Everyone had its beginnings in 1993 when the Department of Education at William Woods University received its first Eisenhower Mathematics and Science Grant to provide three-week training sessions for practicing teachers in mathematics and science education during the summers of 1993 and 1994. The program, Mathematics and Science Teacher Education Resources (M.A.S.T.E.R.), focused on techniques for helping students (especially female students) in the third- through eighth-grade levels. Forty classroom teachers participated in each of the 1993 and 1994 summer sessions.

Initial Collaboration

The M.A.S.T.E.R. Project was deemed a success by the participants who offered suggestions for the future direction of similar mathematics and science education training opportunities. Comments regarding the appeal of using technology as an instructional technique and the challenge of teaching a diverse student population, including students with disabilities and at-risk students, led to the consideration of expanding the technological component of the M.A.S.T.E.R. project with a goal of targeting at-risk students and students with disabilities as the under served population. Focusing on the needs of teachers at the middle- and high-school levels during the 1995-1996 projects seemed a natural progression from the primary and middle level focus of the 1993-1994 projects.

The Annual Special Education Conference planning committee, comprised of the special services directors from three Callaway County public school districts, one county superintendent, the director of a resource center on deafness (Missouri School for the Deaf), and the William Woods University special education faculty member who serves as the Annual Special Education Conference coordinator continued to discuss the curricular and instructional needs of secondary special education students in science and mathematics. Subsequent documentation from the Eisenhower Mathematics and Science Inservice Needs Assessment supported the need for a broader base of instructional delivery techniques. Moreover, the planning committee concluded that the use of technology in the classroom must be included among the new pedagogical techniques. Finally, the committee noted that district wide mathematics and science education goals of the county school districts included improved student achievement and emphasized the integration of higher order analytical and problem solving skills. Ultimately, the committee concluded that effective curricular reform could only occur with increased teacher understanding reflective of a merger of deeper subject matter knowledge with new pedagogical techniques inclusive of technology.

As the final step in the grant proposal process, the chair of the William Woods University Department of Education personally collaborated with the superintendents of the four Callaway County School Districts and the assistant superintendent for instruction at the Missouri School for the Deaf. All future partners supported the concept for the project and the projected content of the Science And Mathematics Are for Everyone project. The proposal was authored by the department chair and the special education faculty member, submitted to the Missouri Coordinating Board for Higher Education, and funded in the amount of $57,940 for the Summers of 1995 and 1996.

The Proposal

The grant proposal addressed instructional issues of at-risk students and special education students who are in regular education mathematics and science classes, as well as the instructional issues of regular education students. Regular classroom and special education teachers at the middle and high school levels were targeted as recipients of the training. The primary focus of Science and Mathematics Are for Everyone was the integration of technology into the existing regular science and mathematics public schools' curricula. This technological focus of the project mandated the linking of the technology to the subject content with the desired outcome of improved teaching and increased learning. Summer workshops were scheduled for a two-week period in June 1995 and June 1996 on the William Woods University campus in Fulton, and two follow-up sessions with participants were also scheduled for each of the subsequent fall semesters.

Objectives for the Science and Mathematics Are For Everyone project were (1) to introduce special education and regular education teachers to the integrated teaching/learning strategies of cooperative learning and use of technology to foster critical thinking; (2) to facilitate special education and regular education teachers to evaluate various teaching/learning strategies with regard to academic content and diverse student needs; and (3) to facilitate special education and regular education teachers to incorporate various teaching/learning strategies into their existing 6-12 curricula.

The Ever-Increasing Collaborative Process

The original proposal called for the teachers to explore such real life issues and experiences in mathematics and science as saving the ocean from pollution, protecting the ozone layer, creating some of the new materials around us, playing basketball, understanding the relationship of the inner body works and health, knowing animals, protecting the environment, using estimation, cooking and baking, keeping a shop, running a hot dog stand, conducting research, and solving problems in general. How to accomplish such a curriculum coupled with up-to-date educational technology and appropriate and creative cooperative learning and problem solving teaching/learning strategies became the impetus for the next stage of collaboration.

This collaborative planning stage involved three special educators from three of the county public school districts, one county superintendent, the director of a resource center on deafness (Missouri School for the Deaf), the educational technologist from the local school district, two university liberal arts professors (one in biology and one in mathematics), two university professors of education, two university librarians, and one outside consultant (a science and mathematics curriculum coordinator from a large, metropolitan school district).

Collaboration for the 1995 summer session began in early fall 1994. The Annual Special Education Conference planning Committee began to promote the project among their teachers on an informal basis. During the Annual Special Education Conference in February, formal registration was encouraged. Simultaneously, the university faculty and librarians were working in tandem with the local school district educators, the educational technologist, and the outside consultant to develop curriculum for each of the ten days of the project. This collaborative process continued throughout the academic year up to the first day of the first project.

The collaborative process presented several difficulties to be overcome. First, bringing together such a large and diverse group created scheduling problems. This constraint was met by meeting in smaller groups involving the project directors and specific individuals working on one aspect of the project, such as the project director and the assistant project director meeting only with the curriculum specialists or only with the technology specialist or only with the district representatives or only with the outside consultant.

The second problematic issue was that the Missouri curriculum standards and frameworks were in various stages of development and available only in draft form throughout the project planning phases. In order to choose topics and courseware for the summer sessions, the science and mathematics professors were introduced to Missouri's developing mathematics and science standards and frameworks initially and had no choice but to stay current with revisions throughout the planning year and even throughout the two weeks of the project time itself. The professors also endeavored to weave the national mathematics and science standards into the project's curriculum, but that attempt also proved challenging in the area of science since those national standards are being bantered back and forth between the two national professional organizations for science education. Occasionally, the biology professor had to return to the Missouri Key Skills and Core Competencies which are currently in place if no clear direction could be provided by either the national standards or the draft version of the Missouri curriculum frameworks.

The third and most problematic area involved the technology itself. The logistics of obtaining compatible courseware, as well as finding the time to preview the courseware, became continuing challenges. The greatest area of concern in preparation for the first year of the project, however, was matching the technological requirements of the courseware with the capability of existing equipment. The need for hardware with greater capacity became apparent. Acquisition of additional Macintosh computers and access to IBM platform computers, as well as a color LCD overhead projection panel, a videodisc player, and a large screen television were necessary. The William Woods University librarians became invaluable resources during this phase of the planning process.

The Project Unfolds

Twenty-eight educators from the local and county schools attended the first year of Science and Mathematics Are For Everyone. Twenty-one were enrolled in the mathematics strand, fourteen in science strand. Seven participants were enrolled in both strands. The total enrollment consisted of eighteen regular education teachers, eight special education teachers, one full-time substitute, and one director of special services. Nearly half of the participants enrolled as a regular education—special education team. Most taught children in sixth grade or above; however, five teachers taught third, fourth, of fifth grade.

Teachers were surveyed before the two-week session regarding their self-perceived computer literacy. On the pre-assignment, given a scale of 0 to 10, four people rated their computer competency as 6, 7, or 8, indicating above average skills; five people rated their skills as a 5 or average, and sixteen teachers considered their computer skills in the below average range—rating themselves between 4 and 0. Accessibility of computers was also surveyed. Based on their responses, ten of the teachers have either an Apple GS or IIE available to them in their classrooms; nearly an equal number have either an IBM compatible platform (six) or Macintosh (seven); three indicated that they do not have a computer in their classrooms or one readily available, and two did not respond to the query.

Six-hour sessions involving both the science and the mathematics participants were conducted on Day 1 and Day 6. The workshop on Day 1 focused on critical thinking, cooperative learning, and technology. This session was provided by Tom Snyder productions and set the stage for the remainder of the project's activities. The workshop on Day 6 focused on image processing and was presented by the Center for Image Processing. This session introduced the science and mathematics teachers to the teaching/learning strategy of image processing and pertinent applications in the teaching of science and mathematics.

During Days 2-5 and 7-10, the science and mathematics strands were conducted separately. The daily format for these days was generally organized so that one third of the class time was spent addressing each of the three project objectives: (1) introduction to the technology, (2) evaluation of the technology, and (3) integration of the technology.

Generally speaking, a class session proceeded in the following way. During the first one-third of the session, the educational technologist introduced the function and use of the technological strategies to the participants. He had primary responsibility for the first one-third of each three-hour session. The project director and the assistant project director interacted with the educational technologist by relating the software and other courseware to Missouri's science and mathematics curriculum frameworks which are currently in draft form.

The next one-third of each session involved the participants' working in their cooperative groups (1) to gain hands-on experience with the day's technological teaching/learning strategy, (2) to evaluate this teaching learning strategy with regard to academic content and diverse student needs, and (3) to begin to devise strategies for integrating the technology into their own curricula. The educational technologist helped the participants with the hands-on part of the technological experience, and the project director, the assistant project director, and the liberal arts professor of biology or mathematics helped to facilitate the discussion and evaluation concerning academic content as related to diverse student needs and Missouri's curriculum frameworks.

The final one-third of each session required the teachers to work in their cooperative groups to brainstorm ways in which the software, other courseware, and the teaching/learning strategies demonstrated during that day could be incorporated into their respective existing 6-12 curricula. During this time, the educational technologist, the subject area specialist, the project director, and the assistant project director were able to interact with the participants, and the participants were able to continue their hands-on experiences with the technology.

Following is the class format for one science session as it appeared in the participants' syllabus:

9:00-10:00

Use of a video camera attached to a microscope for demonstration of pond water organisms will be demonstrated. Mr. McElroy [the educational technologist] will demonstrate the software The Protozoa, Photosynthesis, and Dinosaurs. Participants will be able to examine the video camera and its applications and access the software programs as time and equipment availability permit.

10:00-10:45

Dr. Spratt [biology professor] will evaluate and relate this software to national academic standards and the proposed Missouri curriculum frameworks. This particular program fits into the Science Competency and Key Skills: (A) Life and Living Things.

10:45-11:30

Participants will work in their cooperative groups to brainstorm strategies for incorporating this software into their respective curricula. Particular emphasis will be placed on strategies for helping "at risk" students. Participants may continue to work with the technology as time and equipment allow.

11:30-12:00

Dr. Spratt [biology professor], Dr. Tutt [project director], Ms. Foley [assistant project director] will facilitate whole group sharing to include questions and answers from all participants. This activity should ultimately lead to evaluation of the usefulness of this particular software, each package of which is suitable for differing age levels/abilities, with regard to academic content and diverse student needs.

In addition to specific instruction on the use of specific subject area software, such as those described above and participation in the One Computer Classroom and Image Processing presentations which have been previously described, both classes received instruction on using the Internet, accessing The Guide for Math and Science Education Reform (a database which lists resources for mathematics and science education), and using Inspiration (a brainstorming program). The science strand was introduced to physiology probes, connecting a microscope to a computer, and simulation software, such as Visi-Frog, Sim Life, and Sim Earth. The mathematics strand viewed and discussed courseware for teaching algebra, geometry, and statistics. Mathematics participants previewed and explored classroom applications for other courseware, such as Hot Dog Stand, Mathblaster Mysteries, and the Jasper Woodbury series.

Six weeks from the conclusion of the project each teacher or group of teachers was required to provide the projector director with four descriptions of how the technological strategies presented during the two-week session would be or could be incorporated into her/their curricula during the ensuing school year. The following information was required to be a part of these descriptions: activity or unit title; name(s) of participant(s); targeted grade level; subject area, for example earth science; topic, for example earthquakes; description of content or process skills which would be learned or associated with the activity or unit; size of student work group; instructional strategy(ies); number of class periods required to complete the activity or unit; introduction to and overview of the activity or unit; statement of desired learning outcomes; requisite technological resources; classroom procedures; evaluation procedures and instruments; background of the activity or unit to provide the reader with information required before public school students attempt to conduct and/or participate in the activity or unit; and a description of the natural curricular extensions and connections of the activity or unit. Finally, the participants' activities or units were required to incorporate (1) some courseware demonstrated during Science and Mathematics Are For Everyone, (2) procedures relevant to the development of knowledge and skills mandated by state and national standards, and (3) appropriate adaptations for students with special needs into existing science and mathematics curricula.

Accountability

The outside consultant for the project developed assessment instruments and procedures for program evaluation and assessment of participants' technological knowledge and skills. Before the two-week sessions began, participants were sent a pre-assessment instrument which gathered general information and included questions concerning the participants' teaching styles, the participants' experience with various forms of technology, and the specific criteria the participants typically used when selecting classroom and technological resources. Overall, the pre-assessment instrument revealed the participants' knowledge and understanding of courseware, function and operations within technology instruction, and related terminology to be very limited.

Participants' growth in these critical areas will be finally assessed when they respond to the same instrument as a post assessment at the second follow up session in the fall. Participants also completed a program evaluation of the two-week summer session rating overall satisfaction to topics presented, courseware, presenters, interest level, and format. These ratings were favorable with over eighty per cent of the participants rating the workshop content and their increased knowledge of technology as "high" or "excellent."

However, we believe true success of this project can only be measured by increased student learning in the classrooms of the project's participants. This increased student learning will occur to the extent that the participants (the classroom teachers) develop appropriate adaptations of the technology and relevant teaching strategies for their students. Working to achieve these goals will be the focus of the on-going collaborative planning process for the second summer of our project.